Scenes for Student Actors

Garry Michael Kluger

D1016430

MERIWETHER PUBLISHING
A division of Pioneer Drama Service, Inc.
Denver, Colorado

Meriwether Publishing
A division of Pioneer Drama Service, Inc.
PO Box 4267
Englewood, CO 80155

www.pioneerdrama.com

Editor: Arthur L. Zapel
Typesetting: Angela Greenwalt
Cover design: Tom Myers

© Copyright 1997 Meriwether Publishing
Printed in the United States of America
First Edition

Library of Congress Cataloging-in-Publication Data

Kluger, Garry Michael, 1955-
    Fifty professional scenes for student actors : a
collection of comedy & drama for two performers / by Garry Michael
Kluger. -- 1st ed.
    p.   cm.
    ISBN 978-1-56608-035-4 (pbk.)
    1. Acting--Auditions. 2. Dialogues.
PN2080.K58 1997
812'.54--dc21

97-42106
CIP

2   3   4   16   17   18

To my wife Lori who is my everyday inspiration
and fills my heart and my life.

To our baby, Emily Danielle, who I'm sure
will give me mounds to write about.

And finally this book is dedicated to the memory of Bobby Hoffman.
Bobby was the "actor's friend" but more importantly to me,
my friend and mentor. He gave me the confidence and push to write.
He was one of Hollywood's "good people" and is truly missed.

I would like to thank the following people who have helped or inspired the characters in these following pages come to life:

Lori Oliwenstein-Kluger

Emily Danielle Kluger

Karen Miller

Julie Dolan

Wayne Duvall

Glenn Kelman

Mark Torreso

Splash Kluger

Steve Kluger

Jeff Kluger

Bruce Kluger

David Taavon

Traci Mitchell

Barry Holland

Ira Katz

Steve Gundler

AND

A special thanks to The Allen Fawcett Sound Stage for filming all these scenes and especially Mr. Allen Fawcett who gave me a place to write and made sure quality was always the top priority.

Contents

SECTION TWO
DRAMA

Introduction

The scenes included in this book were written over four years and have been filmed by over 250 actors and actresses all over the country. They have also been performed in theatres, classes, showcases and have been used in auditions for all the major networks from coast to coast. They are the most used *original* audition scenes in Los Angeles. In other words, people like them.

I am writing this introduction because I want the actors and actresses who use this material to be aware of a couple of things. These scenes differ from the ones in my first book, *Original Audition Scenes for Actors* in that they are, for the most part, gender non-specific. Meaning that they can be performed in any combination of actor and actress that is desired. The dialog appears in a specific form. Instead of a line like, "He went to the store" or "She went to the store," what you would see is "He/She went to the store." The pronoun used would depend on who is being spoken about. The same applies to a line like, "My husband is great" or "My wife is great." It would appear as, "My husband/wife is great." Then it would depend on who is speaking.

Lastly, I have been a writer for a long time and an actor even longer and what I've found is that no matter what the scene, drama or comedy, you have to enjoy the experience. These scenes can be sad, funny, poignant, and sometimes very dramatic, but they should still be FUN to perform. Please get all the excitement out of these scenes that you can while you perform them. That will help to make you all better actors and actresses.

Enjoy,

Gary Kluger

P.S. I'd love to hear any comments or stories you might have about these scenes. You can leave me a message at **gmk15@aol.com**

Section One:

COMEDY

1. Santa's Helpers

(We are in a coffee room. #1 is seated at a table going over some notes. #2 enters and sits next to #1.)

#1: How's everything going out there?

#2: Terrific. They're just putting the finishing touches on Santa's house now. The whole mall looks really great. This is costing a fortune. How'd you get them to spend all this money?

#1: Easy. I waited until the last minute and appealed to all the shop owners' most basic holiday instinct.

#2: Greed?

#1: You bet. I convinced them that any mall could put up a little chair for Santa, but if they all chipped in and helped create "Santa's Village," statistics showed that their businesses would all increase three-fold by Christmas.

#2: Where did you get your statistics?

#1: I made them up.

#2: You didn't?!

#1: No, actually, I didn't. I took this year's buying trends, the GNP figures, the current value of the stock market, the latest interest rates, crunched all the numbers, and interpolated.

#2: And you came up with triple business figures?

#1: Actually, it came out to one-and-a half.

#2: Then why did you say business would triple?

#1: I did the calculations twice and got $1^1/_2$ both times and...

#2: $1^1/_2$ plus $1^1/_2$ equals three.

#1: See how easy?

#2: That's not very honest.

#1: Come on, no one was hurt. Our company made more by creating "Santa's Village." You said yourself it looked great. A lot of kids will come, and if the store owners do ten percent more than last year, they'll be happy. Everyone wins.

#2: I'm still not sure.

#1: I am so relaxed. Now, what's the schedule?

#2: They should finish putting everything up in an hour. The reindeer arrive at nine. Nice touch, by the way.

#1: Thanks.

#2: Santa should arrive at nine-forty five, and the mall opens at ten. The radio commercials will jump to every hour and from what I understand, the projections show a big crowd.

#1: That's the news I wanted to hear. So, who's playing Santa?

#2: You tell me and we'll both know.

#1: What do you mean?

#2: What do you mean, "what do you mean?"?

#1: I mean, are you saying you didn't hire a Santa?

#2: No.

#1: This is news I didn't want to hear. Why not?

#2: Because you said that you'd take care of it.

#1: When did I say that?

#2: Yesterday. I was supervising the house building, you came over and asked what I had left to do. I said ordering Santa. You got a call, while you were answering the phone I asked if you wanted me to get the Santa now and you said, "no, I'll take care of it."

#1: I wasn't talking to you. I was telling Sheila back at the office. I was telling her I'd take care of the press people.

#2: How was I supposed to know that?

#1: This is great. Santa's Village with no Santa. Don't you see something fundamentally wrong with that?! Get on the phone and order us a Santa. NOW!

#2: OK, I'll try. *(Takes out a cellular phone and dials.)* **Good morning. This is James/Joan with Gateway Entertainment Group. We've created "Santa's Village" at the Coast Mall and we need a Santa.** *(Pause)* **Stop laughing, I'm serious.**

6

We need a Santa. *(Pause)* I know it's the start of the season, but... *(Pause)* Yes, but... *(Pause)* When? *(Pause)* OK, do that and... *(Pause)* I'll get back to you on that. Good-bye.

#1: What's up?

#2: We've got a Santa.

#1: Great!

#2: By this afternoon... maybe, but definitely by tomorrow.

#1: What about this morning? Call them back.

#2: It's the start of the season. There's not a Santa to be had and that was the best agency in town.

#1: I don't believe this.

#2: They did say they had a Barney who could fill in until we got a Santa.

#1: Why would I want Barney Rubble...

#2: Not Barney Rubble - Barney the dinosaur. You know, that big purple thing that the kids love.

#1: This is Santa's Village not Jurassic Park. These kids want to sit on Santa's lap, not line up to be a hot lunch for some odd-colored T-Rex.

#2: Can we open tomorrow?

#1: No, all the advertising says today. We've got to find someone. *(Pause)* Well, there's only one solution.

#2: What?

#1: You'll do it.

#2: Are you talking to me?

#1: You see anyone else here?

#2: There'd better be because you're out of your mind if you think I'm putting on that suit...

#1: You have to.

#2: Give me one good reason why.

#1: Greed.

#2: How's that?

#1: You like money?

#2: Only when I need to buy something.

#1: Want to continue making any, 'cause we won't if this

7

doesn't open today?

#2: Whoa, hold on. This was your baby. I'm just the assistant.

#1: But both our names are on this. If it blows up, you think they'll just fire me?

#2: I don't even look like Santa.

#1: *(Tosses some items to #2.)* We have a fat pad and a big red suit. You'll be great.

#2: What would you say if I told you I was Jewish?

#1: Happy Chanukah, St. Nick. Get dressed!

#2: Do you know how much I hate this?

#1: Do you know how much I don't care?! Just think of this as your Christmas present to all these kids.

#2: Very funny. Ha, ha, ha.

#1: No, it's Ho, Ho, Ho. Remember that.

#2: Merry...Christmas. You remember that. *(Takes the suit and exits.)*

#1: I forgot. James/Joan, do you know where we can get an elf?... *(Runs off after #2.)*

2. The Actors

(We are in the waiting room of a casting office. #1 is sitting quietly, eyes closed preparing for an audition. #2 enters, looks around, signs in, sits next to #1, picks up a magazine and starts to read and hum. After the humming (or singing) gets louder #1 opens his/her eyes and turns to #2.)

#1: Excuse me. My contemplative silence isn't bothering you, is it?

#2: *(Looks up at #1.)* I'm sorry, are you talking to me?

#1: Keen grasp of the obvious you have there. Yes, I'm talking to you.

#2: What can I do for you?

#1: I am trying to prepare and your singing/humming, at least I assume it's singing/humming, is interrupting me.

#2: I'm sorry. I'll be quiet.

#1: Thank you.

#2: My pleasure. *(#1 closes his/her eyes. Just as he/she gets settled...)* So what are you preparing for?

#1: *(Opens his/her eyes.)* Since I'm sitting in a casting office, my first guess would be...an audition.

#2: Oh. *(Looks at the script #1 is holding.)* Hey, look at that. We're auditioning for the same part.

#1: How nice for us. And I suppose that sparks feelings of kinship for you, hmm?

#2: No, I was just making small talk.

#1: Please don't. I'd like to prepare. I need to center myself.

#2: Please, go right ahead. Forget that I'm here.

#1: From your mouth... *(#1 closes his/her eyes and starts to center. #2 turns and watches and slowly moves in very close. After a beat, #1 opens his/her eyes.)* **What are you doing?!**

#2: *(Jumps.)* You scared me. I...was just watching you center. I've never seen anyone do that before. You didn't even move.

#1: Of course I didn't. When you center it's not physical. It's internal.

#2: Oh, I see. Where did you learn that?

#1: From Uta.

#2: Oh, so it's one of those Eastern Religious things.

#1: What? *(Pause)* No, I didn't say Buddha, I said *Uta.*

#2: Oh. *(Pause)* What's an Uta?

#1: Where were you raised? She's not a what. She's one of the greatest acting teachers that ever lived. You've never heard of Uta Hagen?

#2: No, I haven't. Was she ever on "Roseanne"?

#1: How long have you been acting?

#2: A little over a year.

#1: And you're here. Amazing. During my first year of acting I wasn't allowed to audition. I wasn't even allowed to talk.

#2: Why?

#1: Because until I understood my craft, until I could start to create a character, what I had to say as an actor was irrelevant. I wasn't worthy of being heard.

#2: Who told you that?

#1: Stella.

#2: Stella? Let me guess, Uta's sister?

#1: Where exactly did you study acting?

#2: What's to study? They give you things to say, and you say them. Seems pretty straightforward to me.

#1: It would. Do you want to see how it's done professionally?

#2: Sure. Sounds like fun.

#1: Fun? FUN?! Acting is not fun. It's an art and art is suffering. It's digging down into the depths of your soul and despair. It's reaching down and grabbing that inner most secret part of yourself, wrenching it out and laying it bare for the world to see and trample on. The one thing it's not...is fun! Understand?

#2: *(Gets a little tentative.)* **Yeah. I understand.** *(Pause)* **Boy, you take this acting stuff seriously, don't you?**

#1: **Do you want to do this or not?**

#2: **Yeah.**

#1: *(Gets up.)* **OK, stand up.** *(#2 stands.)* **Now close your eyes.**

#2: **Why?**

#1: **Because you can't connect with your inner self if you are connected to the outer world. If you can see the outer world, you are connected to it.**

#2: **Makes sense. OK, I'll close my eyes.** *(Closes his/her eyes.)*

#1: **Now spread your arms wide.** *(#2 starts to speak.)* **Don't ask why. Just do it.** *(#2 does.)* **Now, I want you to let your feet and legs become one with the floor, your body one with the air, and your mind one with the universe.**

#2: *(Opens one eye and looks at #1.)* **You're spreading me a little thin, aren't you?**

#1: **What?**

#2: **Well, it's kinda hard to become one with anything with my mind in the universe, my body in the air and my feet on the floor.**

#1: **You're missing the point. This is to free you up so you can dive into your character and pull its heart out.**

#2: **I don't want to pull its heart out. I just want to read what he/she is supposed to say.**

#1: **But until you understand this person, how can you portray him/her?**

#2: *(Picks up his/her slides.)* **This is a dog food commercial. All I have to understand is that this person has a dog, Rex, who likes Mr. Woo's Chinese Dog Food.**

#1: **This is my point, and Uta's. If that's all you know, you've just scratched the surface. If you don't explore more than that, how do you ever expect to get a job?**

#2: **Oh, I've gotten jobs. I've done some commercials.**

#1: How many commercials could you have possibly gotten?

#2: Last year...fourteen.

#1: FOURTEEN!?

#2: Is that a lot?

#1: It's...OK. What were they? Those little local things?

#2: No, they were shown all over the country. My agents said they were called...um...

#1: Nationals?

#2: Yeah. That's what he called them.

#1: You did fourteen national commercials last year?

#2: Uh-huh. They were fun, too. I made enough to put a down payment on a house.

#1: Well...until you learn more, I wouldn't expect that to last too long.

#2: Tell me about it. Since the beginning of this year, I've only done three.

#1: But it's only February.

#2: I know. Last year at this time I had done five.

#1: *(Sits down, dumbfounded. Then finally...)* So...tell me... what exactly do you do when you audition?

#2: Well I...wait, what about Uta and Stella?

#1: Forget them!

#2: Why, I thought they were the best.

#1: Did they ever do fourteen national commercials in one year? You bet they didn't! So tell me.

#2: OK. See I walk in there...

3. The Ad

(#1 is pacing around a conference room. He/she looks at a watch, then picks up a phone and dials.)

#1: Is he/she in? *(Pause)* I know that he's/she's supposed to be with me, but he's/she's not. Well, if he/she gets back kill him/her for me and send him/her over. *(#2 enters.)* Never mind, I'll kill him/her myself. He/she just walked in. *(Hangs up the phone.)* Where have you been? Your meeting was over an hour ago.

#2: Do you know what it's like trying to get a cab from downtown at this hour?

#1: Never mind that, did we get the account?

#2: Yes...

#1: We did?! That's great!

#2: Sort of.

#1: Sort of? You think it's only "sort of" great we got the account.

#2: I didn't say that. You didn't let me finish. It's not sort of great, we only sort of got the account.

#1: How can you sort of get an account?

#2: Well, it's come down to us and A & F Advertising.

#1: What? Not A & F. I hate those guys. They always beat us out.

#2: I know, that's why I beat them to the punch.

#1: *(Pause)* How?

#2: *(Sits.)* OK, you'll love this. We're in the office of Matt Simmons, the vice president of Chunky Cookies. It's Peterson from A & F and me. Now, Simmons says that Chunky wants a whole new direction and what have we got. Peterson says they have some ideas, and they'll be able to put something together by Friday. That's when I jumped in. I said that we've already been working on it

13

and Simmons says that he wants to see what we've got.

#1: When?

#2: Tomorrow.

#1: Tomorrow?! Are you nuts?! We haven't got anything.

#2: I know that, but they don't.

#1: But they're going to think we're crazy tomorrow when we bring them in blank pages.

#2: Look, do you want us to be a minor league ad agency forever? If we're going to get ahead we have to take some chances.

#1: A & F has five times the people we do. They will be ready on Friday. Everyone here left for the day and we need a team if we we're going to have a full campaign by tomorrow.

#2: You're not listening. They don't want a full campaign, just an outline of where we're going. You and I can do that. We did start this company, you know.

#1: Yeah, I know, and if I remember correctly, you were the one who talked me into leaving that great big firm and starting our own.

#2: And we've done pretty well so far.

#1: I know, but now we're hitting the big leagues. I don't want to blow it.

#2: We won't.

#1: OK. Did Simmons give you any clue as to what they wanted?

#2: Let me check my notes. *(Pulls a pad out of a briefcase and reads.)* Yeah, he said he wanted the campaign to be... good.

#1: That's it? Very specific. For that you had to check your notes?

#2: I wanted to make sure I got it right.

#1: So, what do you see as our outline?

#2: OK, Chunky is like the fourth biggest cookie company. So how about "We're #4, but we try harder."

#1: That's good, and after the Avis Car Company sues us, what then? No, see you're missing the big picture. What's your first impression of Chunky Cookies?

#2: They stink!

#1: What?

#2: They're terrible. They taste like compressed dirt with little pebbles in them.

#1: But do kids like them?

#2: Of course they do. You could take a piece of asphalt, cover it with chocolate, call it a jaw breaker and kids would eat it. It doesn't mean I'd let them.

#1: Wait a minute. What did you just say?

#2: Uh...you could take a piece...

#1: No, after that. About not letting them have it.

#2: Well, I wouldn't. There so many preservatives in it, embalmers are trying to get the recipe.

#1: That's our angle.

#2: Unhealthy ingredients as an angle?

#1: No, parents not letting kids have the cookies. And why? Go ahead, ask me why.

#2: OK, why shouldn't parents give the cookies to their children?

#1: Because they're too good for kids. They should be for adults only.

#2: Didn't some cereal company do that already?

#1: Sort of. They said their cereal was not only for kids. Adults liked it, too. What we're saying is that kids shouldn't even be allowed to have them. The cookies are too grown-up.

#2: You're joking. What's that going to do?

#1: Come on, think! You know what kids are like. The moment you tell them they can't have something...

#2: They want it all the more.

#1: Exactly! And the kicker is, some of those brain-dead, adult, couch potatoes will see the ad, believe it, and they

#2: We could show a father going into a study, opening a wall safe and pulling out a bag of cookies.

#1: Oh, how about this? *(Does the action as he/she explains.)* We show an elegant dinner party. You know, champagne, the whole nine yards, but instead of waiters with trays of caviar, or hors d'oeuvres, the trays are full of Chunky Cookies.

#2: And we could show the kids sneaking downstairs and stealing cookies from the trays.

#1: Yes, this could work! Listen to this one. We show a kid in the market. He's at the checkout counter and he hides the Chunky Cookies under some other items. The checker starts to ring up the stuff...

#2: ...notices the cookies, stops and asks "You got an I.D. for that, son?"

#1: And the kid says, "No, ma'am" and the checker says...

#2: "I'm sorry, these are for adults only." This is great. We can even do one for the farm kids. We can show a kid sneaking out of the house. She yells back inside, "I'm going to milk the cows, Ma." She sneaks into the barn and pulls a bag of Chunky Cookies out, looks around to make sure the coast is clear, and starts to eat them.

#1: These ads could run forever. *(Pause)* Oh no, we're going to need a slogan. You know Simmons is going to want that tomorrow. *(They both start to think.)*

#2: OK, we're going for that adult cookie thing?

#1: Yeah.

#2: Fine, then we do like the movie ratings. We say, "Chunky Cookies, the only cookies rated A. For adults only!"

#1: I like it. Let's get some of this down on paper before we forget. *(They grab some pads and start to write. #1 stops.)* Are they really that bad?

#2: *(Pulls out a bag of cookies, gives #1, one. He/she takes a bite* and spits it out.) **Pretty bad, huh?**

#1:   **They stink!** *(Pause)* **The kids'll love them.**

4. The Aunt

(Scene Opens: We are in a living room. #1 comes in and starts looking around. #1 then goes to the middle of the room and stops.)

#1: OK! Enough of this! I know you're in here.

#2: *(Off-stage)* I am not. That's just a rumor.

#1: Then how come I can hear you?

#2: Because this is a pre-recorded message. *(Pause)* Beep.

#1: *(Goes over to the couch, sits, then reaches behind and pulls #2 up.)* What a surprise to find you here.

#2: So you found me. Hooray for you. Now let me go 'cause I'm still not going.

#1: Why do you do this every time we have to go visit Aunt Ethel?

#2: I'll give you three guesses.

#1 You don't want to go?

#2: Bingo! Got it on the first try. Have a nice day. *(Starts to exit.)*

#1: STOP! Get back here. *(#2 slowly comes back.)* Explain to me why you don't want to go.

#2: Will it make any difference if you understand?

#1: No.

#2: Then why should I tell you?

#1: Because I like to watch you squirm.

#2: I'm so happy I can amuse you.

#1: Just tell me why you don't want to visit Aunt Ethel.

#2: Well, to start, I always have to hug her when I see her.

#1: So?

#2: So...she's...gigantic. She just doesn't hug me, she squeezes me. She like one of those big wrestlers on T.V.

#1: *(Starts to laugh a little.)* OK, I know. She is a little...large.

#2: A little?! Arnold Schwarzenegger is smaller than she is.

#1: I get the point. Anything else?

#2: Well, I have to kiss her...

#1: And she's got a mustache.

#2: I wasn't going to say that.

#1: You don't think she has a mustache?

#2: No. I think she's got a beard. She looks like Santa Claus.

#1: You shouldn't say that.

#2: You asked me.

#1: You're right, I did, didn't I?

#2: Yeah, you did and I didn't even mention her house, yet.

#1: What's wrong with her house?

#2: It smells and it's full of old things.

#1: Well, she's old.

#2: But does everything she has have to be old, too?

#1: Try and understand. All those things she has at her house are the things she's collected during her life. A lot of the stuff she got when she was a little girl and some of the furniture was given to her by her parents, so of course it's going to be old. What did you think was going to be there? Power Rangers and Ninja Turtles?

#2: No, but she might have a T.V.

#1: She does. It's in that big cabinet in the living room.

#2: That's the cabinet I'm not allowed to touch, right?

#1: Right.

#2: See, I can't win.

#1: I know. Now about the smell...

#2: Yeah, why does it smell like that?

#1: Once somebody gets to be a certain age, their house always seems to smell that way. I think it's a law. *(#2 laughs a little.)* Look, I know going to visit Aunt Ethel isn't your favorite thing to do on a Saturday. When I was your age I didn't want to go see her either.

#2: Do you now?

#1: No, not always, but she is family.

#2: So is Uncle Norman and we never visit him.

#1: Uncle Norman lives in Alaska. You're stretching here.

19

#2:   Hey, it was worth a try.

#1:   All I'm saying is that Aunt Ethel is our family matriarch.

#2:   Our what?

#1:   She's the oldest woman in our family...

#2:   You can say that again.

#1:   Just listen. She's the oldest woman in our family and she's earned our love and respect. When you get to be her age, won't you want your family to visit?

#2:   I suppose.

#1:   She loves us and wants to see us. Is that really so tough for you to do?

#2:   No.

#1:   Good. Then we'll go see her and you'll smile and be nice to her.

#2:   Can I at least bring her a razor?

#1:   Go change!

       (#2 exits. #1 watches and laughs.)

5. The Body

(We are in a police station. #1 is sitting at a desk, filling out some reports. #2 enters. #2 appears a bit....distracted.)

#1: How's it going?

#2: SHHHH!

#1: What...what's wrong?

#2: Nothing's wrong. What could possibly be wrong? Did somebody say something was wrong?

#1: No. I just took an educated guess. Are you OK?

#2: No, something's wrong.

#1: What?

#2: We...is anyone else here?

#1: Do you see anyone?

#2: No.

#1: Then by deductive reasoning, I'd say we're alone. What's the matter with you?

#2: I'm having a slight problem with the interrogation.

#1: I knew it! Is that little weasel refusing to talk?

#2: Well, yes and no.

#1: What do you mean, "yes and no"? Did he talk or not?

#2: Well, I got him to confess, told him that if he testified against Gianelli we'd cut him a deal, he agreed, then...

#1: Did he sign the confession?

#2: Yes and no.

#1: Again with yes and no? Did he sign it or not! *(#2 hands #1 the paper. #1 looks it over.)* He only signed his first name.

#2: I know that.

#1: He didn't sign his last name.

#2: I know that, too.

#1: Why didn't he sign his last name?

#2: He can't.

#1: He can't or he won't?

#2:   He can't.

#1:   He can't?

#2:   He can't!

#1:   Why not?

#2:   He's dead.

#1:   What do you mean, "he's dead"?

#2:   I mean he's dead.

#1:   What do you mean, "he's dead"?!

#2:   I MEAN HE'S DEAD! He stopped breathing. He ceased to exist.

#1:   Please tell me you're making this up.

#2:   I wish I was.

#1:   I cannot believe you killed our witness!

#2:   I didn't kill him! He just died.

#1:   No one "just dies."

#2:   Well, he did.

#1:   What happened?

#2:   I'm not sure. We were talking, he agreed to everything... oh, then he asked me for a glass of water and I told him as soon as the confession was signed. He took the paper, started to sign it, grabbed his chest and bam! Keeled over. *(Pause)* Maybe I should've given him the water first.

#1:   I really don't think that would have made a whole lot of difference. *(Pause)* This is not good.

#2:   You figure that out all by yourself?

#1:   Hey, I wouldn't be a smart-aleck if I were you, considering the fact that you're the one who killed him!

#2:   I DIDN'T KILL HIM!

#1:   Whatever. The point is, he's dead! OK, does anyone else know about this yet?

#2:   No.

#1:   Good! Let's try and keep it that way.

#2:   Don't you think someone might get a little suspicious after a week or two. I mean with the smell and everything...

#1: Just until we can figure out what to do. *(Pause)* **The problem is — no one, no, let me rephrase that, no news person is going to believe that this "wanted criminal" just happened to die while in our custody. Not after all the statements we've made about how much we hate these guys. The department's going to look real bad.**

#2: Never mind the department, what about us? *(The phone rings. They just stare at it.)* **Oh, you don't think it's the captain, do you?**

#1: No. Our luck couldn't be that bad. *(Answers the phone.)* **Dawson.** *(Pause)* **Hi, Captain.** *(Covers the mouthpiece and talks to #2.)* **Yes it could.** *(Goes back to the phone.)* **What can I do for you, Captain?** *(Pause)* **It's going as well as can be expected.** *(Pause)* **Problems? I wouldn't say there any real problems.** *(Pause)* **NO! I don't think it would be a good idea to send in anyone else.** *(Pause)* **Why not? It would, uh...** *(Signals #2 to help.)*

#2: Uh...make him nervous.

#1: Yeah, it would make him nervous.

#2: He's used to just us.

#1: Yeah, he's used to just us. *(Pause)* **Oh, that's just Crawford.** *(Pause)* **He/She is watching the prisoner. He/She just came out to get him a...pick-me-up. See, the prisoner's a little...**

#2: Dead.

#1: Dead,...tired!! Dead tired. *(Pause)* **Yes, sir. We'll have that confession any minute now. We're...just hammering out the last few details.** *(Pause)* **OK. I'll call you the minute we have it.** *(Hangs up and puts his head in his hands.)* **We are in trouble!** *(Pause)* **Let me see that confession again.** *(#2 hands #1 the confession.)* **OK, as I see it, all we have to do is get him to finish signing this.**

#2: Is that all? What do you suggest? A seance or should we wait until he's reincarnated, and have him sign it then?

That's assuming he doesn't come back as a cow or something.

#1: Just pay attention. He already signed his first name, all we have to do is sign his last. Simple.

#2: That's forgery. It's a crime.

#1: Why? We're only signing his last name.

#2: So we'd only be committing a half a crime. Great. That's so much better.

#1: You want those other guys to walk?

#2: No.

#1: We're not making anything up. We need this and Martelli was signing it. We're really not doing anything wrong.

#2: Then you sign it.

#1: Forget it! That's forgery.

#2: We're sunk.

#1: No, wait! I just had a thought. Is he still holding the pen?

#2: I think so.

#1: Great. Sit down. *(#2 sits at the desk. #1 gets a folder and goes over to #2.)* Look here's Martelli's signature. He wrote his last name with an **M** and a squiggle. *(#1 demonstrates as he/she tells this.)* Just take his hand with the pen and have him make the **M** and squiggle. Then we wouldn't be lying when we say he wrote it with his own hand. See, all legal.

#2: You're really stretching on this one.

#1: Our only other choice is to tell the Captain we blew a two-year investigation and our star witness is dead.

#2: Not a good alternative.

#1: No, it's not. Then when you're done, we'll take the confession to the Captain, suggest he talk to Martelli himself, we'll all go in there and "discover" him.

#2: Won't the department still be in trouble?

#1: Possibly, but we won't be.

#2: Good point. *(Pause)* OK, Give me the folder. *(#1 hands #2 the folder.)*

#2: *(#2 gets to the door and looks back.)* **I should have been an accountant.**

(2 exits. #1 watches, then when #2 is gone, #1 sits at the desk, puts his/her head in his/her hands and mumbles to himself/herself.)

#1: **God I hate police work.**

6. The Break-In

(We are in a darkened office. We hear a rattle and the door opens slightly. We see a beam of light. #1 partially enters with a flashlight. He/she looks around and looks back.)

#1: **The coast is clear. Come on.**

(#1 enters all the way followed by #2, who also has a flashlight.)

#2: **Don't bury yourself in the role.**

(They both shine their lights around the room.)

#1: **OK, let's check over there by the desk.**

(They head to opposite sides of the desk and start looking around.)

#2: **Do me a favor, tell me again why we're doing this.**

#1: *(Shines the light in #2's eyes.)* **Fine, why...**

#2: **Get the light out of my eyes.**

#1: *(Puts the light down.)* **Sorry. Now, why are we doing this? How many ad campaigns have we come up with in the last couple of months?**

#2: **Five.**

#1: **How many has Sam Tyler come up with?**

#2: **Five.**

#1: **How may were exactly the same?**

#2: **Five.**

#1: **I rest my case. We know he's stealing our stuff. We just want to prove it.**

#2: **And how do you know that he's going to hand in our latest idea?**

#1: **I heard him telling Florence in the lunch room today he was handing in this big campaign idea tomorrow. Right when we've finished ours. You do the math.**

#2: **OK, fine. Let's find the file, learn the truth, and get the hell out of here.**

#1: **Ten-four.**

#2: What?

#1: A-OK.

#2: What?!

#1: I agree.

#2: Then just say that!

#1: OK, I'm sure Sam's hidden the file in a safe behind one of these pictures, so let's take them all down. *(Starts taking a picture down.)*

#2: *(Looks in the desk.)* Hey!

#1: Don't bother me, I'm busy.

#2: Why don't we just check the desk first?

#1: Because it's too obvious. No one would hide a file in their own desk.

#2: *(Pulls a file out of the desk drawer.)* Ta-daa! Here it is. Campaign idea for Power Top Shoes.

#1: *(Grabs the file.)* Let me see that.
(They both look at the file.)

#2: Well, it is our idea.

#1: I told you so. We'll take this and confront Sam tomorrow.

#2: Great. Can we get out of here now?

#1: Ten-four... I mean sure. I'll make sure the coast is clear. *(Goes to the door and peers out.)* Oh, no!

#2: What? What's wrong?

#1: A security guard's out there.

#2: So, we'll wait until he leaves.

#1: I don't think so.

#2: Please, don't think, it only gets us in trouble. Tell me what you know.

#1: It's Big Rollie and he's set up a chair and it looks like he's planted his big butt for the night. He even brought food.

#2: Well that's great! What do we do now, genius?

#1: *(Looks around.)* No problem. We'll go out the window.

#2: Did you major in moron in college? We're on the thirtieth floor! Who do I look like, Batman?! "Come Boy Wonder/Batgirl, we'll leap 300 feet to the ground and make away with the file."

#1: It was just a suggestion.

#2: Yeah, a stupid one.

#1: Well, I don't hear you come up with any better ideas.

#2: Why don't we just talk to Rollie and tell him the truth.

#1: What, that we broke into Sam Tyler's office? Rollie takes his job very seriously. He thinks he's Elliot Ness. *(Pause)* But...maybe we could rush him.

#2: He weighs like 400 pounds. I don't think so. I guess we're stuck in here until morning or until Rollie falls asleep or dies!

#1: Wait! That's it!

#2: What, wait till he dies?

#1: No, the man weighs 400 pounds. We use that to our advantage. We'll cover our faces and run for the stairs. He's the only guard here. He'll never catch us. We'll race down the thirty floors and out the back.

#2: That'll set off the alarm.

#1: Sure, but we'll be long gone before the cops get here.

#2: I am not going to do some half-baked Starsky and Hutch episode with you.

#1: Where is your sense of adventure?

#2: I left it in my other suit. You don't get it, do you? These are our jobs you're messing around with. We could blow our whole careers here. All the days we've worked. All the nights we've put... *(Stops in mid-sentence.)*

#1: What?

#2: Did you hear what I just said? We work a lot of nights.

#1: So?

#2: So, all we have to do is turn on the lights, start talking, walk out, and tell Rollie we were working late.

#1: And what do we tell him if he asks what we're doing in Sam's office?

#2: That our computer was down and we were using his. We see Rollie here all the time when we work late. There's nothing unusual about this.

#1: But...

#2: But what?

#1: *(Thinks.)* But...nothing. You're right.

#2: I know. *(Pause)* Come to think of it, there was no reason to sneak in here in the first place. We could have used the elevator.

#1: I know, but wasn't scaling that wall and climbing the fire escape great?

#2: I was right, you are a moron. Let's get out of here. *(#1 and #2 start to exit.)* I really can't believe how stupid I was.

#1: Me, either.

#2: I can. See, for me it was a once in a lifetime thing. For you it's an everyday occurrence.

#1: Hey, was that a cut?...

7. The Exchange

(The exchange department of a large store. #1 enters carrying a coffee maker. He/she goes to the counter. No one is there. There is a button that says "Ring For Assistance." #1 rings. Nothing. He/she rings again. Nothing. And one more time. Nothing. Finally #1 calls out.)

#1: Excuse me! *(Pause)* Hello! Is anyone here?
(We hear #2 Off-stage.)

#2: Yeah, I hear you. Can you wait a minute?

#1: *(Yells back.)* Not really. I'm sort of in a hurry.

#2: *(Enters.)* I'm sorry. We just got a television back and I was checking something out.

#1: Are you the repair person?

#2: No.

#1: Then what were you checking out?

#2: Oprah. She's doing this show about transsexual accountants who want to marry their pets. Right now she's talking to some guy, who used to be a girl, who's in love with his French poodle and...

#1: I'm sure it's very interesting, but I do have another appointment.

#2: Right. So...what can I do for you?

#1: Well, I was given this... *(Puts the coffee maker on the counter)* ...and I don't like it.

#2: Oh.
(Silence. The two just stare at each other.)

#1: Aren't you going to say anything else?

#2: Umm... I'm sorry you don't like it?

#1: *(Pause)* This is the exchange department, isn't it?

#2: Do you want to exchange this? Why didn't you just say so?

#1: Isn't it obvious? Why else would anyone come here?

#2: Gift wrapping sometimes.

30

#1: You do gift wrapping here?

#2: No, the next office over.

#1: Then why would anyone come here for gift wrapping?

#2: Sometimes people get confused. Like you are.

#1: I'm not confused. If I thought this was gift wrapping, I would have asked for gift wrapping. True?

#2: True, but if you thought this was the exchange department, you would have asked for an exchange. All you said was that you didn't like this.

#1: And what does that sound like to you?

#2: A complaint. That department's on the third floor.

#1: OK, let's start over. I got this coffee maker, I don't like it, and I'd like to exchange it.

#2: Why?

#1: I just told you, I don't like it!

#2: That's it?

#1: Isn't that enough?

#2: Not always. I don't know if "I just don't like it" is covered in our store's exchange policy.

#1: Look...

#2: Now just stay calm and let me check. *(Picks up a large binder.)*

#1: What's that?

#2: The rules and regulation for exchanges.

#1: All that!? How difficult can an exchange be?

#2: You'd be surprised. Now let's see... *(Starts thumbing through the book.)* "I just don't like it"...ah, here we are. "Rules covering, 'I just don't like it.'"

#1: You're joking? They actually have a rule on that?

#2: They sure do. See? *(Shows #1.)*

#1: *(Starts to read.)* "Customer just doesn't like it. See Complaint Department." What does that mean?

#2: *(Snaps the book shut.)* It means that you have to go upstairs to the complaint department.

#1: And what happens there?

#2: Usually, they'll listen to you and send you to the exchange department.

#1: BUT I'M ALREADY AT THE EXCHANGE DEPARTMENT!

#2: I know, but you didn't go through proper channels!

#1: OK, what if I tell you I was already at the complaint department and they sent me here?

#2: Then you'd have a complaint - slash-exchange transfer slip. Do you?

#1: *(Defeated)* No, I don't.

#2: Then you'll just have to go upstairs to be sent where you are now.

#1: Look, I know that you have rules, but is it at all humanly possible that you could show just a hint of compassion?

#2: Compassion? I don't know. Let me check. *(Opens the binder again and starts thumbing through it.)* Let's see... compassion. Ah, here we are. *(Reads.)* Hmm, very interesting.

#1: What?

#2: Well, it appears that in an extreme case I am indeed allowed to act in what might be referred to as "the customer's best interest." It's a judgment call. But is this an extreme case?

#1: Oh, yeah.

#2: Why?

#1: Because if I don't get some help, I'm pretty sure I'm going to rupture a blood vessel in my head, causing uncontrollable psychotic behavior that will result in the death of anyone in the near vicinity. Now, what would you classify that?

#2: Extreme! Let's take care of this for you.

#1: Thank you.

#2: All I need is your receipt.

#1: My what?

#2: Your receipt? Don't tell me you don't have one.

#1: No, it was a present. My friend gave this to me and said if

I didn't like it to exchange it here.

#2: Then get the receipt from him.

#1: I can't. He went to Bangkok on business today.

#2: My you do seem to have a peck of troubles, don't you?

#1: So you won't exchange this? Extreme situation, remember.

#2: I know, I know, but no receipt, no exchange. Now if it was a defect, that's a different story.

#1: Really? How's this? *(Rips the cord of the machine.)*

#2: You broke it!

#1: I know! Now, it's a defect. So what's the story on that?

#2: Uh... defects don't come here. They have to be sent back to the manufacturers.

#1: But you said...

#2: I said defects were a different story. You didn't let me finish. You have no one to blame for your predicament but yourself. And before that blood vessel thing happens, I think I'll go to lunch. Have a nice day.

(#2 grabs his/her binder and runs. #1 is standing there with the cord in his/her hand.)

#1: I should have stayed home. *(Just walks away dejected.)*

8. The Hereafter

(We are in a room. #2 is seated in a chair, apparently asleep. #1 is in a chair next to #2. #2 stirs and wakes.)

#1: Hi.

#2: *(Tentative)* Hi.

#1: How are you feeling?

#2: Fine...I think. Where am I?

#1: Is that really important?

#2: I think so.

#1: OK. You are where you are.

#2: *(Pause)* Thanks. Is there any reason I shouldn't know?

#1: No. It's just kind of hard to explain, first thing.

#2: Try.

#1: What's the last thing you remember before you woke up here?

#2: *(Thinks for a moment.)* I was leaving work.

#1: Keep going.

#2: I left my office...got in my car...put on my headphones and started driving home. After that I'm drawing a blank.

#1: Then let's go to the videotape. I always wanted to say that. Makes me sound like a sportscaster. *(Pushes a button and we hear the audio of a car crash. #1 stops the tape.)* Didn't anyone ever tell you not to drive with headphones on? It's very dangerous.

#2: That's odd. That...that looks exactly like me.

#1: There's a good reason for that. It is you...or should I say was you.

#2: What do you mean, "was"? Define "was."

#1: "Was: Verb. Middle English from the Old English" meaning...you ain't an "is" anymore.

(#1 and #2 look at each other and both start to laugh.)

34

#2:   That's very funny. No, Seriously, what was that?

#1:   Seriously? Your death scene. It wasn't as dramatic as say...Hamlet's, but it did have a certain...flair to it. Especially that final explosion.

#2:   I don't believe you.

#1:   No, you all never do. Just once I'd like to tell someone that they're dead and have them say, "OK, where do we go from here?"

#2:   Well, I apologize for being skeptical, but I wake up in a strange place, with a strange person telling me I'm dead.

#1:   I'm not strange.

#2:   I don't mean strange...weird. I mean you're a stranger. Who are you?

#1:   Let's just say, I'm the office manager for lack of a better description.

#2:   OK...and you want me to just accept that fact that I'm dead because you say so?

#1:   Well...yeah.

#2:   Why should I?

#1:   Because you are. Believe me, you bought the farm, checked out, shuffled off this mortal coil...

#2:   I get the picture. OK, assuming for the sake of brevity that I did...

#1:   Die?

#2:   Yeah. Aren't you being a tad on the...insensitive side about it.

#1:   Hey, I don't have the time to try and convince you. What do you think, you're my only appointment today? Things could go a lot faster if we didn't have to do the standard "No, I'm not...yes, you are" banter.

#2:   But it's impossible. I'm too young to be dead.

#1:   Hey, let me clue you in on something, when one drives off a freeway overpass doing sixty-five, age has very little to do with it.

#2:   But I've got a lot more to do. More to accomplish.

#1: Not in that life you don't. They can stick a fork in you 'cause you're done.

#2: Isn't there anything I can do? Some...deal I can make?

#1: Sure. How much money you got?

#2: *(Starts frantically looking for cash, then pulls out a check book.)* Will you take a check?

#1: I was kidding.

#2: So you don't make any deals?

#1: Who am I, Monty Hall? Besides, I don't make deals with dead people. No percentage in it.

#2: So...I'm really...dead?

#1: Yes, you're really dead. You wanna see the tape again?
(#1 starts to push the remote button. #2 stops him/her.)

#2: NO! I believe you. *(Pause)* I'm dead!

#1: I know.

#2: So...where do I go from here?

#1: That's better. I don't know. I really can't answer that...precisely.

#2: What can you answer...precisely?

#1: Nothing. The final decision is up to the big guy. You're his next appointment.

#2: Does everyone meet with him?

#1: No. Some people get sent right along. Most, like you, have to be evaluated.

#2: Why do I have to be evaluated?

#1: Honestly? You had a dumb death. The boss doesn't like to send those on without a meeting first.

#2: He thinks my death was dumb?

#1: Well, what would you call catapulting off the freeway into oblivion with country western music blaring in your ears? Noble?

#2: No, but...

#1: Still, it was better than, say, drowning in a bowl of Jello.

#2: *(Pause)* Somebody actually did that?

#1: Hard to believe, huh?

#2: And what exactly happens at this meeting?

#1: You sit, you talk, then it's decided what's done with you.

#2: "What's done with me"? What are the options?

#1: They vary.

#2: Name some.

#1: OK. Some people stay here if the boss thinks they'll be useful. Then, some people are sent back to complete their lives. Some are...

#2: Wait! Are you saying that some people are put back into their old bodies?

#1: Yes, but...

#2: No, buts! I like that one. Let's do it.

#1: Sorry, can't do that.

#2: Why?

#1: First, it's not my decision. Second, if I could, there'd have to have been a body to put you into. You blew up, remember? There's not much left except maybe a random finger or toe, and I don't think you'd want to spend the rest of that life as a toe, do you?

#2: No, not really.

#1: See the problem? So, if you are sent back, it's decided what form you're sent back in.

#2: Is there a possibility I might be sent back as an animal?

#1: Or a fish or maybe even an insect....

#2: I could come back as a spider?

#1: If that's what the boss needs.

#2: I don't want to be a spider!

#1: Have you ever been one before?!

#2: Not that I know of.

#1: Then how do you know you wouldn't like it?

#2: But...see...I...it would...

#1: Look, just go into your meeting and stop worrying. Everything in the universe is done for a reason. The boss knows what's best. You wanna second guess him?

#2: No.

#1: Didn't think so. You also don't want to keep him waiting. It's your turn. Just go right through that door.
(#2 gets up and starts to exit. He/she stops at the door and turns back to #1.)

#2: I do have one last question.

#1: What?

#2: You keep saying "the boss." Who's the boss and which ...way did I go?

#1: Let's just say, you got what you deserved.

#2: It's going to be a long eternity. *(Exits through the door.)*

9. The Hostage

(A warehouse. #1 is pacing. #2 comes around the corner while taking off a mask and joins #1.)

#1: What's he doing?

#2: Eating.

#1: Again? That's what, four times this morning? He's a skinny old man. Where the heck does he put it?

#2: I don't know. He says he's hypoglycemic and he'll faint if he doesn't eat something every hour. Have I mentioned what a mean son of a gun he is?

#1: Not since his last feeding. Well, we'd better make this call now or any money we get for him will go to food. You got the phone?

#2: Yeah. Here it is. *(Pulls out a cellular phone.)*

#1: Where'd you get it?

#2: Fat Mike sold it to me.

#1: Fat Mike? Fat Mike's a pickpocket.

#2: So?

#1: So, that thing is probably hot.

#2: We kidnapped an old man and were about to ransom him. Dealing in stolen merchandise is pretty much of a step backwards for us.

#1: Forget I said anything. What are you going to say?

#2: How's this. *(Takes out a piece of paper and prepares to read some copy. As he/she does, he/she uses a phony voice.)* We've got your father. If you want to see him again...

#1: Wait a minute, wait a minute. What's with the voice?

#2: I'm disguising it so no one will recognize it.

#1: Who do you think you are, Frank Sinatra? Your voice is hardly a recognizable entity.

#2: What?

#1: Nobody knows you!

39

#2: Excuse me, but you seem to forget that I worked for that family.

#1: You delivered flowers there...once. Two years ago. Get a grip.

#2: I still think I should change it.

#1: Be my guest, just pick another voice.

#2: Why?

#1: Because we want to be taken seriously. What you're doing makes it sound like their uncle was kidnapped by a cartoon.

#2: I'll change it, but what do you think of our demands?

#1: I don't know. You have to read them to me. *(#2 prepares to read.)* And for now, just use your real voice.

#2: We want one million dollars in small, non-sequential bills. We will call you back tomorrow and explain the plan for delivering the money.

#1: What plan?

#2: I think we should run whoever is going to deliver the money all over town before they leave it in the trash bin.

#1: Why?

#2: So we know they're not being followed.

#1: *(Pause)* You saw "Dirty Harry" again last night, didn't you?

#2: Well...

#1: Well, nothing. We're not running anyone anywhere. Just have them drop the money at noon. The trash is picked up by the city at 12:30. We'll get it then. Just tell them that we'll be watching. If we see anyone following the truck, then the deal's off.

#2: That's so boring.

#1: Make the call!

(#2 dials the phone and listens.)

#2: It's ringing. *(Pause)* Hello. I think you've been expecting our call. We have your uncle... *(Pause)* I said, we have your uncle... *(Pause)* Hello, hello? They hung up.

#1: What do you mean they hung up?

#2: They answered the phone, there was a lot of noise...

#1: What kind of noise? Like a bad connection or something?

#2: No...actually, it sounded like they were having a party. Anyway, I said "we have your uncle," they said "what"? I said "we have your uncle," they said "good" and hung up.

#1: You idiot! You must have dialed the wrong number.

#2: Not too likely.

#1: Give me the phone. I'll take care of it. *(Takes the phone, dials, and waits.)* Hello...I said, hello! *(Pause)* You might be able to hear me better if you turned the stereo down. *(Pause)* It's a live band? Then tell them to take ten! *(Pause)* Thank you. Now, we have your uncle and if you... *(Pause)* I mean we're the ones who kidnapped him... *(Looks stunned.)*

#2: What's the matter?

#1: *(Into the phone)* Hold on. *(To #2)* I told them we kidnapped their uncle and they said, "thank you." What is going on? You talk to them. *(Pushes the phone to #2.)*

#2: Hello. *(Pause)* I'm not sure you heard us right. We said that we kidnapped your uncle. *(Pause)* Stop thanking us. If you want to see him alive then you'll give us one million... um... I said one million... uh *(Pause)* you want to stop laughing?

#1: Give me that! *(Grabs the phone back.)* Look, maybe you don't get what we're saying. We have your uncle. He's old and frail and... *(Pause)* OK, he's old and frail and nasty, but.... *(Pause)* you know, we're not going to get anywhere if you keep calling him names. If you want to see him alive again, you'll... *(Pause)* What do you mean you don't want to see him again? *(Pause)* Why not? *(Pause)* You people are pretty sick. We'll call you back.

#2: I'm afraid to ask.

#1: You should be.

#2: What did they say?

#1: They said he's a mean, horrible, nasty man that no one

really likes, but they're all still in his will, so keep him.
They don't want him back.

#2: This isn't good.

#1: Well, there's only one thing to do. *(Pulls out a gun.)* You
have to kill him.

#2: Come again?

#1: You have to kill him. *(Pushes the gun on #2.)*

#2: Why me?

*(#2 pushes the gun back. They keep pushing the gun back
and forth as the dialog continues.)*

#1: Because he's seen you.

#2: No he hasn't. I always wore a mask around him. Just like
you.

#1: Oh...then...this was your idea.

#2: It was your idea.

#1: You...keep saying how mean he is and how he kicks you
every time you give him food. You hate him.

#2: Obviously so does everyone. If you're so hot on killing
him, you do it.

#1: I can't. I've never killed anyone before.

#2: And who am I, Charles Manson? I've never killed anyone.

#1: So what do you suggest we do?

#2: Look, he's old. Maybe if we go in, wave the gun around,
make a lot of noise, like we're gonna shoot him he'll get
scared and have a heart attack. *(Pause)* What do you think?

#1: *(Pause)* I think you're a moron.

#2: Well, I don't hear you coming up with any bright
suggestions. How about if we just leave. After we're gone
we'll call the cops and tell them where to find him.

#1: I can't believe that we're not going to get anything out of
this. *(Just then we hear an Off-stage voice of the old man
yelling. #1 gets an idea.)* Wait, I have an idea. Where's that
phone? *(Finds the phone and dials.)* Hello, it's us again.
(Pause) Nice to hear you, too. Look, we have your uncle...
(Pause) Wait! If we don't get one million dollars by four

o'clock, he'll be back at your front door by 4:05. *(Pause)* Now, don't panic. We'll give you time to get the money together. *(To #2)* I knew there was an answer.

#2:   I still think we should run them all over town.

(We hear another Off-stage voice of the old man.)

#1:   You wanna take care of him? *(Back to the phone)* Yes, I hear you. We want small bills...

10. The House

(An empty house. The CLIENT is looking around while the REALTOR checks some notes.)

REALTOR: Well, it seems that this house has everything you're looking for.

CLIENT: Yes, it does. I love that oak paneled den. It'll make a great home office.

REALTOR: One of the former owners used it for the same thing.

CLIENT: What can I say. The place is perfect.

REALTOR: Then why don't we go back to the office and start on the paperwork.

CLIENT: Fine. *(The REALTOR pulls out some papers for the CLIENT to sign.)* I still can't believe this place is going so cheap. I thought it would be at least 25 percent more.

REALTOR: Well...it is a very soft market right now. The owners aren't looking to make a big profit.

CLIENT: Tell me, what's the history of this house?

REALTOR: Didn't you get the information sheet when we came by the first time?

CLIENT: No, I didn't.

REALTOR: Oh.

CLIENT: I know that I was supposed to. Can you fill me in now?

REALTOR: Sure. Let me see if I have that information. *(Looks through some files.)* OK...uh...here we are. *(Starts to read.)* Let's see. The house was built in 1939. All the foundation has been checked over the years and it's as solid as ever. There was some earthquake damage in the basement in 1953 and that was fixed. In 1961, the new owners added on the back part of the house. In 1973 a triple murder/suicide was committed here. In 1979 all the wiring was replaced and the plumbing was redone in '85. In...

CLIENT: Wait...wait...you wanna back up and repeat that for me.

REALTOR: The plumbing was redone in 1985. It was old and really in need of...

CLIENT: No. Before that.

REALTOR: The wiring was redone in '79.

CLIENT: I think you know which one I'm talking about.

REALTOR: The triple murder/suicide?

CLIENT: Bingo! Tell me, were you planning on just sliding that one by me?

REALTOR: No, not at all. It's just that...with a house this old, it's hard...uh...to remember everything that's happened here. Especially an...unfortunate little...mishap.

CLIENT: "An unfortunate little mishap"?! And how do you refer to the Titanic? An unfortunate little hole with some water damage?

REALTOR: Please don't get carried away. When the Marstons lived here...

CLIENT: The Marstons?! This is where the Marston murder took place?

REALTOR: So you know about it.

CLIENT: After a book, two miniseries, a feature film, a Broadway play and an opera, it's kinda hard not to. That was the kid who chopped up his mother, father, and grandmother, switched all their limbs, then killed himself.

REALTOR: See, people are always exaggerating. *(Pause)* He only switched two arms.

CLIENT: That makes me feel so much better. No wonder this place is going so cheap.

REALTOR:	It's still a great house.
CLIENT:	And just how many owners has this great house had since "the little mishap"?
REALTOR:	*(Pause)* Twelve.
CLIENT:	Twelve!?
REALTOR:	OK, thirteen, but the last one didn't count since escrow never officially closed.
CLIENT:	And they all left because of the Marston murder.
REALTOR:	No. They knew about it when they bought the house.
CLIENT:	So why leave?
REALTOR:	There were several reasons.
CLIENT:	Oh, just pick your favorite.
REALTOR:	OK...do you believe in the supernatural?
CLIENT:	I think I hate this. Why do you ask?
REALTOR:	There have been some reports of...occurrences.
CLIENT:	What kind of occurrences? Are you saying that this place is haunted, too?
REALTOR:	Haunted is such a generic word. Let's just say that...things have happened.
CLIENT:	What kind of things?
REALTOR:	Well, objects being moved...
CLIENT:	You mean like a lamp floating across the room or something?
REALTOR:	No, more like the entire house being redecorated overnight. But quite tastefully from what I understand.
CLIENT:	Terrific. Anything else?
REALTOR:	A few sightings and...
	(All the lights go out.)
CLIENT:	Don't tell me, let me guess. An illumination problem?
REALTOR:	We thought it was the wiring, but it was all replaced.
	(The lights come back on.)

REALTOR: See, it doesn't last very long.
CLIENT: Very reassuring. So who is doing the haunting...
            (SFX: wind, screams, running down the stairs, etc.)
REALTOR: We think it's the Marstons.
CLIENT: That should about do it!
            (We hear a voice.)
VOICE: GET OUT!
CLIENT: And apparently he agrees with me. Bye. *(Starts to exit.)*
REALTOR: What about the house?
CLIENT: What?! I really hope you don't think I'm going to buy it now!
REALTOR: Well, you did leave a non-refundable deposit.
CLIENT: That's because you didn't tell me about any of this.
REALTOR: Well how would you have had us list it? As a "beautiful three bedroom, two-and-a-half bath, complete with den, built-ins, lurid past and highly disturbed ghost"?
CLIENT: You know, that's not my problem. Just get me my money back. *(Goes to the door, but it's locked.)* You want to unlock the door? Please.
REALTOR: It's not locked.
CLIENT: Then why won't it open?
VOICE: BECAUSE I DON'T WANT YOU TO LEAVE.
CLIENT: But you said....
VOICE: SHUT UP. I'VE CHANGED MY MIND. DO YOU LIKE MY HOUSE?
CLIENT: Well...I...
VOICE: ANSWER ME!
REALTOR: I wouldn't antagonize him if I were you.
CLIENT: Yes, I like the house.
VOICE: THEN BUY IT OR I'LL FIND YOU WHEREVER YOU ARE!
CLIENT: But...

VOICE:	**BUY IT! SIGN THE PAPERS NOW!**
	(The REALTOR opens the folder and the CLIENT signs.)
CLIENT:	**OK?**
VOICE:	**NOW – GO!**
	(The CLIENT opens the door and runs. The REALTOR looks around and smiles.)
REALTOR:	**Thanks, Mr. M.**
VOICE:	**MY PLEASURE.**
	(The REALTOR puts the folder away and exits.)

11. The Job

(Scene in an office. Seated behind the desk is JUDITH. She is an office manager for a large company. JUDITH is, to say the least, a strong woman. She is no-nonsense and the kind of person who isn't afraid to say what is on her mind. At present, she is on the phone.)

JUDITH: No, you listen to me. You are the ones who call yourselves an employment agency. You have sent me fifteen incompetents to interview for my assistant. I have one more of your people to interview and if this one is no better then the rest of the dweebs you've sent me, I'm going to come down there and rip out what you laughingly refer to as your heart. Do I make myself clear? *(Pause)* Thank you. Have a nice day. *(She puts down the phone and pushes the intercom.)* Brandon, send in the next one. *(Goes back to some work on her desk as GLENN enters. GLENN is a nice, pleasant man in his late 20s. He walks up to the desk and stands there. JUDITH doesn't look up. There is a pause.)*

GLENN: Ah-hem.

JUDITH: Do you need instructions on how to sit?

GLENN: No.

JUDITH: Then do it.

(GLENN sits. JUDITH still doesn't look at him. GLENN waits a few seconds.)

GLENN: Well, hi there. I'm Glenn.

JUDITH: *(Finally looks up.)* Do you have a last name or are you going for that Fabian, Liberace kind of thing?

GLENN: It's Keller and you are...

JUDITH: God...as far as this office is concerned.

GLENN: I see. It's nice to meet you. *(Pause)* How's your son?

49

JUDITH: *(Cracks the faintest of smiles.)* **Is that a joke?**

GLENN: **I suppose that depends on whether you laugh or not.**

JUDITH: *(Pause)* **Good answer. I'm Judith. Let me see your resumé.** *(GLENN hands it to her. She reads it over.)* **You seem to have a lot of experience. Why did you leave your last job?**

GLENN: **The company I was working for had financial difficulties and was forced into bankruptcy.**

JUDITH: **Did you have anything to do with it?**

GLENN: **Of course not!**

JUDITH: **Just checking. Let me explain what would be expected of you here. This is an extremely busy company and I have a lot to take care of. You would be my assistant. Have you ever worked for a woman before?**

GLENN: **I used to do chores for my mother when I was a kid. Does that count?**

JUDITH: **Are you trying to be clever?**

GLENN: **Well, If you don't mind my saying, you seem a bit tense. I'm just trying to ease the situation.**

JUDITH: **The reason I'm tense is that I can't seem to find an assistant with an IQ higher than that of a gumdrop.**

GLENN: **How many assistants have you had?**

JUDITH: **Eight.**

GLENN: **Today?**

JUDITH: **It seems like it. I need someone who will be satisfied working for me. I need someone who won't have to be told everything, can anticipate what I need or what has to be done, won't question me, and when I say "jump" will answer "how high?"**

GLENN: **I'm a little confused. Are you looking for an assistant or a eunuch?**

JUDITH: **You're cocky, aren't you?**

GLENN: **No, I just don't intimidate that easily.**

50

JUDITH: Do you think I'm trying to intimidate you?

GLENN: Honestly...yes.

JUDITH: You haven't seen anything, yet.

GLENN: Why don't you just cut out all this preliminary stuff then and just stick some bamboo shoots under my fingernails.

JUDITH: Meaning?

GLENN: Meaning, this isn't an interview. It's a police interrogation. Now why don't you try asking me some pertinent questions and cut out the tough act.

JUDITH: Finished?

GLENN: *(Pause)* Yes, I think so.

JUDITH: Good. Now it's my turn. All this may seem like an act to you, but if you had to deal with all I do and have had to interview as many imbeciles as I have, you might be able to understand why I interview the way I do. For all I know, you might crack under the pressure.

GLENN: I don't crack under pressure.

JUDITH: As far as I can tell you're cracking right now, just being interviewed.

GLENN: Oh, I see. You act like this and you're being thorough, but I give it back and I'm cracking under the pressure. Have you ever thought that you might be the one losing it?

(The conversation starts to get loud now.)

JUDITH: OK, listen to my mouth! You are never going to meet a more together lady in your life. You should get down on your knees and give thanks that I even allowed you to walk into this office. To be allowed to work for me would be a blessing from heaven for you.

GLENN: Who are you kidding!? Working for you should be a sentence imposed by a court for breaking some law. Of course that would probably constitute cruel and unusual punishment.

51

JUDITH: **Keep it up and I'll show you cruel and unusual punishment.**

GLENN: **Who are you, Vito Corleone? What are you going to do, press the intercom and get Luca Brasi in here to throw me out?**

JUDITH: **Don't flatter yourself. I wouldn't bother my staff for such a trivial disposal.**

(They are leaning across the desk almost nose to nose.)

GLENN: **You know lady, you have some serious problems. You don't need an assistant, you need a keeper.**

JUDITH: **And you need to find the door.**

(Silence.)

GLENN: **I'm outta here.**

(They stare at each other for a few more seconds, then GLENN turns and heads for the door. Right as he gets there, JUDITH yells for him.)

JUDITH: **HEY!**

GLENN: **WHAT!**

JUDITH: **YOU START MONDAY!**

GLENN: **FINE!**

JUDITH: **NINE O'CLOCK!**

GLENN: **OK!**

(He storms out and she goes back to work.)

12. The Jumpers

(On the ledge of a building. #1 is standing there. Obviously not in the best mood, #1 is contemplating his/her next (and probably final) move. #1 yells out.)

#1: I told you all to go away! I'm not doing this for your entertainment. *(To him/her self)* I thought this was supposed to be a private moment.
(Just then #2 enters on the ledge. #1 & #2 are looking in opposite directions. Finally they spot each other, scream, start to lose their balance and finally catch themselves.)

#2: Ahhh! You scared the hell out of me!

#1: You?! What about me?! You almost made me fall.

#2: Well...you should have been watching.

#1: Who are you? I told them not to send anyone up here. I said I'd jump if they did.

#2: Fine. Go ahead and jump. I'm not up here to save your sorry butt.

#1: Then who are you and what are you doing up here?

#2: *(Pause)* I was in my office and it looked liked such a nice day that I thought I'd go for a walk. *(Pause)* What do you think I'm doing here?

#1: You're planning on jumping?

#2: Nothing gets by you, does it?

#1: Well I'm sorry. You can't. At least not here.

#2: *(Looks at #1.)* And pray tell why not?

#1: Because I was here first.

#2: What are you saying, this is a "first come, first jump" ledge? Fine, go ahead. Far be it from me to steal your thunder.

#1: That's not the point! I'd like to be alone. Why don't you go somewhere else.

#2: I was somewhere else. I was on the other side of the building.

53

#1:   So what are you doing here?

#2:   It got too crowded on the street over there. Plus, they kept yelling "Jump! Jump!"

#1:   Really? They haven't done that here.

#2:   How long have you been out here?

#1:   About half an hour.

#2:   Give them another fifteen minutes. They'll start. They get bored if there's no action. That's why I came here.

#1:   Well, you can't stay. I can't do this if somebody is watching.

#2:   Who do you think's down on the street. A convention of blind people?

#1:   That's different. They're...not in the immediate vicinity.

#2:   Yeah, well, live with it! I'm not moving.

#1:   *(Pause)* As long as you're here, I suppose it's OK if you stay.

#2:   How nice. You're letting me stay. What are you, the Mayor of the ledge?

#1:   Boy, you're not very nice.

#2:   I'm sorry. I've had a lousy day.
      (There is a silence as both #1 & #2 look around. #2 notices something from far below.)

#1:   I think they're yelling something. Can you make it out?

#2:   Yeah, they're yelling "Jump!" I told you they'd start.

#1:   Maybe it's just the people that followed you.

#2:   Whatever.

#1:   You know, that really is pretty sick. Don't those people have anything better to do?

#2:   Apparently not. What do you expect? It's just another day in the "big city."

#1:   They're probably the same jerks who stop on the freeway to gawk at an accident. *(They both chuckle a bit. Then there is a silence.)* So, why are you up here?

#2:   You gonna write my life story?

#1:   Oh, come on. If you tell me why you're here, I'll tell you why I'm here.

#2:   Great. I'm literally about to jump into the great beyond

54

and I'm gonna spend my last minutes on earth playing, "I'll show you mine, if you show me yours."

#1: Never mind! Forget I said anything.

#2: OK, I'm sorry. Why are you up here?

#1: My girlfriend/boyfriend dumped me.

#2: And?

#1: And...nothing.

#2: Nothing. You're going to kill yourself because you got dumped?

#1: Are you saying that's not good enough?

#2: To tell the truth, it is pretty lame.

#1: And I suppose your reason is so much better.

#2: It's not even a contest.

#1: Fine, tell me.

#2: OK, if you want to know so badly. I got up this morning and my cat was run over by a truck, I was mugged and robbed on the subway on the way to work, I just found out my partner embezzled all the funds from our business, my wife/husband just called and told me he's/she's realized he/she is in love with our mail carrier, the IRS wants to audit me, and to top it off, I think I'm getting a cold sore on my lip.

#1: Cold sore?

#2: It was just the final straw.

#1: Wow. That is terrible.

#2: And it's not even lunch time yet.

#1: And you think this is the best way out?

#2: All you did was get dumped and you do.

#1: That's different. It really hurt.

#2: Oh, please. "It really hurt." I can't believe I'm out here with such an amateur.

#1: But I really loved him/her.

#2: And there's no one else out there?

#1: Not like him/her.

#2: Have you looked? *(Pause)* No, I'm sure you haven't. The

first little setback and you want to chuck it all.

#1: **What about you? Things could be worse.**

#2: **Really? Let see, I've got no business, no money, no spouse, probably no mail now, no cat, I'm going to jail, and this cold sore really hurts. Suicide will be the best thing that could happen.**

#1: You know, listening to you, I guess things aren't that bad for me. *(Pause)* Do you really think I can find someone else?

#2: **Let me put it this way, if you jumped right now, you'd probably splatter on twenty or thirty single men/women down there.**

#1: **You know, you're right!**

#2: **Well hurrah for me.**

#1: **No, really. He/she wasn't good enough for me. I can find someone else. Maybe a hundred times better. He/she isn't worth my life.**

#2: **Yeah, yeah, I'm very happy for you, but you want to keep it down. Some of us still have business up here.**

#1: **Are you sure?**

#2: **Yeah, just go.**

#1: **OK, but I'll never be able to thank you enough. You've saved my life.**

#2: **Then shut up before I regret it.**

#1: **OK, I'm going.** *(Starts to inch off the ledge. Then stops.)* **I'll never forget you.**

#2: **Please do. This is not how I'd like to be remembered. Have a good life.** *(#1 exits. #2 turns to see if #1 is finally gone, then reaches into his/her pocket and pulls out a cellular phone and dials.)* **Yeah chief, he's/she's left.** *(Pause)* **Hey, I'm sorry it took long.** *(Pause)* **If you don't like it, find someone else to do this!** *(Pause)* **Yeah, OK. One last question, how do I get down from here?!**

13. The Medium

(In a house. There is a MEDIUM sitting at a table. Peering into a crystal ball and dealing tarot cards.)

MEDIUM: Please enter and feel welcome. *(The CLIENT comes in and looks around.)* **Please, sit down.** *(The CLIENT sits.)* **I am Zolton/Madam Zolton. How can I help you?**

CLIENT: I'm not sure if you can.

MEDIUM: Have you ever sought help from one such as me before?

CLIENT: No I haven't. A friend of mine came to you and suggested I come.

MEDIUM: And who is your friend?

CLIENT: Mary Rogers.

MEDIUM: Yes, lovely Mary. I helped her get in touch with her departed brother.

CLIENT: I know. I was hoping you could help me too.

MEDIUM: I can only do my best. And who do you want to reach Mr./Miss...

CLIENT: Parker. My great-great grandmother. I've been doing some research on my family and I heard she was a fascinating woman. I'd love to see if I could get in touch with her.

MEDIUM: We will do our best. I do have to tell you one thing. To get in touch with someone who passed on several generations ago, is much more difficult than communicating with someone recently departed.

CLIENT: Why is that?

MEDIUM: Those who are longer passed on, are more settled in the afterlife and are not always as willing to reconnect with the living world. It may take a few sessions.

CLIENT: Really? And that will cost me more, I suppose.

MEDIUM: Perhaps, but let's not delve into that until necessary.

CLIENT: OK.

MEDIUM: Now, do you happen to have an article or picture that belonged to your great-great grandmother?

CLIENT: I have an old picture of her.

MEDIUM: Let me have it. *(The CLIENT takes a picture out and hands it to the MEDIUM. The MEDIUM does a meditation, then looks at the picture very carefully.)* This was your great-great grandmother?

CLIENT: Yes, it was.

MEDIUM: She was a very fascinating woman.

CLIENT: You can tell that by feeling the picture?

MEDIUM: No, by looking at it. Why didn't you tell me your great-great grandmother was a First Lady?

CLIENT: I don't...know...what...

MEDIUM: This is a picture of Mary Todd Lincoln.

CLIENT: I...see...no...

MEDIUM: You can drop the act Mr./Ms. Parker. Or should I say... *(Turns over a tarot card and drops whatever accent or voice inflection he/she has been using.)* Officer...Parker.

CLIENT: It's detective.

MEDIUM: Close enough. What do you want?

CLIENT: You in jail.

MEDIUM: Aren't you guys tired of harassing me? I know I'm tired of it.

CLIENT: I want to see you busted. You're a fake and you know it.

MEDIUM: Prove it!

CLIENT: How about Linda Folger?

MEDIUM: Oh, please. That was one person who wasn't satisfied with her results. And, if I'm not mistaken, a court of law backed me up. But you know that, don't you?

CLIENT: People like you make me sick. You cheat people out of their money and you have no guilt about it.

MEDIUM: Hey, I don't promise anything, or guarantee anything. People get exactly what they come here for and they pay me for it. You call it cheating, I call it business.

CLIENT: You're a fake and I'm going to get you.

MEDIUM: Well, until you get some evidence, I think you know where the door is. *(Pause)* Also, I wouldn't be so sure that I don't have any powers. One never knows.

CLIENT: Sell it to someone else.

MEDIUM: That's what I'm planning. Oh, detective, your picture.

(The MEDIUM holds out the picture to the officer. He/She grabs it, but the MEDIUM doesn't let go. They stare at each other for a moment.)

CLIENT: What?

MEDIUM: Nothing. *(The CLIENT takes the picture and starts to head out.)* Don't worry about your dog, detective.

(The Cop freezes and turns around.)

CLIENT: What?

MEDIUM: Your dog, Max. Don't worry. The car didn't really hurt him.

CLIENT: How did you...

MEDIUM: And you should stop worrying about your promotion.

CLIENT: What...do you know about my promotion?

MEDIUM: Just what I felt coming from you.

(The officer walks back to the MEDIUM.)

CLIENT: What do you know about my promotion?

MEDIUM: Why are you asking me? I'm a fake, remember?

CLIENT: Shut up and tell me.

MEDIUM: It's hard to tell. I only got the vibration for a

59

	second. Still, you've got a better shot at that than that car loan you applied for.
CLIENT:	How do you know about that?!
MEDIUM:	The universe is a strange place.
CLIENT:	Tell me more! Tell me more!
MEDIUM:	I can't. I have another appointment now.
CLIENT:	When?!
MEDIUM:	Later. Come back later.
	(The detective starts to head out.)
CLIENT:	I'm off at six. I'll be back then.
	(The detective heads out. The MEDIUM says after he leaves.)
MEDIUM:	Fine. Bring money.
	(The MEDIUM reaches under the table and pulls out a phone and dials.) Hey, it's me. Thanks for the info. *(Pause)* Yeah, the cop looked just like you said. *(Pause)* Your friend at the police department isn't going to tell him you were asking, will he? *(Pause)* Good. *(Pause)* Yeah, yeah, you can pick up your money at the usual time. *(Pause)* Nice doing business with you, too.

14. The Mistake

(In a bank. #1 is a bank manager. He/She is seated behind a desk finishing some work. #1 pushes the intercom.)

#1: You can send in the customer now. *(#2 enters. He/she seems a bit frazzled. Actually irritated would be a better word.)* Please sit down. I'm sorry you had to wait.

#2: Me, too, it's been over an hour.

#1: Well, you know how it is. Paperwork, paperwork, paperwork, makes the world go 'round.

#2: Excuse me?

#1: That's just a little motto we like to use here at the bank.

#2: Really. How nice for you.

#1: I see. You're a bit on the edge today, aren't you?

#2: Just a tad.

#1: Let's see if we can make life a little nicer for you, Mr./Ms....

#2: Collins.

#1: Mr./Ms. Collins, now, what seems to be the problem?

#2: Like I told the other five people this morning, I went to use the ATM and it said to see a teller.

#1: Did you?

#2: Yes. She wouldn't give me any money either. From there I was sent to the sub-assistant manager. Then to the day manager, the afternoon manager, the lunch manager, the upstairs manager, and finally you.

#1: You didn't see Ms. Bickford?

#2: Who is she?

#1: The lobby manager.

#2: *(Pause)* No. *(Pause)* She was sick.

#1: Then I guess "the buck stops here." Now, what seems to be the problem?

#2: OK, once again, I can't get any money from this bank.

#1: Do you have an account with us?

#2: No, I heard that you all just gave away money. Of course I have an account!

#1: Now, let's try and stay calm. Getting snippy won't help anything.

#2: "Snippy"? I passed "snippy" a long time ago.

#1: Then let's get you some answers. What is your full name?

#2: Terry Collins.

#1: *(Types it in the computer.)* Your account number?

#2: 375-282-116

#1: *(Types it in.)* Your address.

#2: 1425 N. Camden

#1: *(Types it in.)* Your mother's maiden name.

#2: Why?

#1: It's for security. We have to make sure this is you.

#2: Caplan. C-A-P-L-A-N

#1: *(Types it in.)* What's your shoe size?

#2: What?!

#1: *(Senses #2 is getting more "snippy.")* Maybe we don't need that. *(Pushes enter.)* Here we are. Oh, I see why you can't make a withdrawal. It's very simple.

#2: Great. What's the problem?

#1: You're dead! I'm glad I could clear that up for you. Have a nice day.

#2: WAIT! What do you mean I'm dead?

#1: According to the computer, you passed away last week. My condolences.

#2: At the risk of sounding "snippy," do I look dead to you?!

#1: It doesn't matter what I see. According to the computer...

#2: It's wrong!

#1: *(Finds this amusing.)* Obviously you don't know the Wang Central Banking Program. It's used worldwide, including Geneva. It's never wrong.

#2: And obviously you're an idiot! I'm sitting here. How can I be dead?

#1: That's really none of my concern. According to Wang, you are.

#2: Well, you can kiss my Wang! Do you know how much money I have in this bank?

#1: *(Checks the screen.)* Yes, I do, but I can only release it to the next of kin.

#2: I'M THE KIN! Release it to me!

#1: I CAN'T. YOU'RE DEAD!

#2: *(Pause)* If you say that one more time, you and everyone in this bank are going to join me in the hereafter.

#1: Are you threatening us?

#2: No, I'm promising you. Besides what can you do to me? You can't arrest a corpse. I'm dead. Remember?

#1: Please, Mr./Ms. Collins. Let's try and stay calm. You can catch more flies with sugar than vinegar.

#2: You give me one more cliché and even an apple a day won't keep the doctor away. For you or Wang. Capice?

#1: Look, Mr./Ms. Collins you have to understand. In the banking world there are two types of dead. Reality dead and computer dead. You unfortunately are the worse of the two. Computer dead.

#2: How is that worse?

#1: If you were reality dead you wouldn't need any money, would you?

#2: *(Pause)* You know, that's the first thing I've heard today that makes any sense. *(Pause)* So what do we do now?

#1: Bring you back to life, I suppose.

#2: Great, and who's in charge of that, the Resurrection Manager?

#1: Who? *(Pause)* Oh, that's a joke. Very good. No, you have to fill out these forms and take them to Mrs. Shearer on the third floor.

(#1 hands #2 a large stack of forms.)

#2: All of these!? By the time I'm done it won't matter. I really will be dead.

#1: Well, bringing you back to life is a complicated procedure.

#2: Obviously more complicated than it was to kill me. So, what am I supposed to do in the meantime for money?

#1: You might try getting a job.

#2: I HAVE A JOB! How do you think the money got in this bank in the first place? The Salary Elf?!

#1: You're getting snippy again.

#2: Look, I have been a good customer here. I work hard, pay my bills, my credit card charges, so there is no reason why I should have to be inconvenienced because you and your stupid computer decided to commit premeditated murder!

#1: OK, you can say what you like about me, but you leave Wang out of it. You have no idea how hard he works. He works 24 hours a day without so much as a "thank you." He is just following orders.

#2: "Following orders"? It's a machine!

#1: How dare you call Wang a machine. That's it! You just take your forms and go upstairs. I don't have to listen to this. Let them take care of you.

#2: FINE! I'd rather be talking to someone who lives on the planet Earth anyway. *(Starts to exit, stops and turns back to #1.)* I hope you and Wang will be very happy together. You deserve each other. *(Storms out.)*

#1: *(Turns back to the computer and starts to type.)* Don't worry Wang, that mean old customer is gone. I hope you didn't hear any of that. You just...

15. The News Broadcast

(In a news studio. #1, a newscaster, is preparing for the evening news.)

#1: **Testing, testing...1, 2, 3. Is that enough?)** *(Off-stage voice: Yeah, it's fine.)* **Then can we get this show on the road?** *(Off-stage voice: Actually, we've got a small problem, Liz/Jim. You're going to have to anchor the show by yourself...again.)* **Forget it! No way! I know what the "little problem" is. Frank/Jane fell off the wagon again, right?** *(No answer.)* **I take your silence as a yes. Well, this amateur stuff has to stop! You all wonder why this station is number five in a three station town. Look, I don't care where you find someone. Just get me a co-anchor.**

#2: *(Enters carrying papers. He/she goes to #1 and hands him/her the papers.)* **Here you go, Ms./Mr. Nance. These are the latest news updates.**

#1: *(Looks #2 up and down.)* **Who are you?**

#2: **I'm Lisa/Larry. I'm the new newsroom intern.**

#1: *(Pause)* **Tell me newsroom intern...can you read?**

#2: **Of course I can read.**

#1: *(Rips the papers out of #2's hand.)* **Congratulations. You've just been promoted. Sit down.**

#2: *(Sits.)* **Wow, things move pretty quickly around here. So what do I get to do? Write the news, I hope? See that's what I really want to be. A writer. I studied writing in college and...**

#1: **Yeah, yeah, that's a moving story, but you're not going to be a writer.**

#2: **Oh, then what am I going to do?**

#1: **You're going to report the news.**

#2: **You mean I go and get the stories, bring them back so you can report on them?**

#1: *(To his/her self)* **Interns.** *(To Lisa/Larry)* **No, you are going report the news with me.**

#2: *(Pause)* **Report the news with you?** *(Panicked)* **From here?** *(Even more panicked)* **ON THE AIR?!**

#1: *(Clips a microphone onto #2.)* **You got it, Ace.** *(#2 turns front, starts to hyperventilate, pulls out a little brown paper bag and starts to breath into it.)* **What are you doing?!**

#2: *(Taking the bag away)* **Hyperventilating.**

#1: **I can see that. Does this sort of thing go on long? See, we're on the air in about two minutes.**
(This causes #2 to hyperventilate faster.)

#2: *(Takes the bag away.)* **I'll be OK. Give me a few seconds.** *(Breathes into the bag and finally calms down and takes the bag away.)*

#1: **Are we calm now?** *(#2 nods.)* **Good. Can we get on with this?**

#2: **Mr./Ms. Nance...I...I can't do this. I can't perform in front of people.**

#1: **Look...Lisa/Larry right?** *(#2 Shakes his/her head.)* **No one is asking you to get up and sing the aria from** *Carmen.* **All I'm asking you to do is read.**

#2: **Read?**

#1: **Yes, you know what reading is. You told me yourself you could read.**

#2: **I know I said that, but...**

#1: **No, no buts, just read. Do you see that monitor, right in front of us?**

#2: **Yes.**

#1: **Well words are going to appear on that and all you have to do is...**

#2: **...read them?**

#1: **EXACTLY! See, you're a natural.** *(To off camera)* **Joe, throw the first story up there for me.** *(Pause)* **Thanks. See the nice pretty words.** *(#2 nods, yes.)* **I want you to read them for me. Can we do that?**

#2: **I think so.**

#1: **Good. Go ahead.** *(There is a few seconds of silence. #1 looks at #2. #2 is mouthing the words and #1 realizes that he/she is reading to him/herself.)* **No, you genius, not to yourself! OUT LOUD!**

#2: **Oh.** *(Pause)* **You don't have to yell. OK,** *(Clears throat - then reads)* **today in Twain, students rioted for five...**

#1: **Stop, stop! Today in Twain? So much for being able to read. I think if you check that again, you'll finds that it's TAIWAN. You know...the island...off the coast of China.**

#2: **I know where Taiwan is. I told you I can't do this. All these people make me too nervous.**

#1: **You can do this! Just forget the people.**

#2: **I can't.**

#1: **Look, do you want to be a sniveling, kowtowing, subservient, little nobody of an intern your whole life?!**

#2: **No.**

#1: **Then I want you to suck it up, and look straight ahead at the monitor.** *(Pause)* **No crying!**

#2: **I'm not.**

#1: **Now, look at nothing else in the room. Are you doing that?**

#2: **Yes.**

#1: **Good. Take a deep breath.** *(#2 does)* **and READ THAT STORY!**

#2: **Today in Taiwan, students rioted for over five hours in opposition to the government's enforced curfew. There were three fatalities and hundreds of people were injured.** *(Pause)* **I DID IT! I really did it. I read that in front of all these people.**

#1: **I told you, you could do it. So, how do you feel about doing it for real?**

#2: **You know, I think I can. I really think I can. This is going to be a piece of cake, a cinch. You know, I bet I could do this in my sleep. I bet...**

#1: **Whoa, Ace. You wanna calm down? How about we**

concentrate on not throwing up on camera for a start, huh?

#2:   OK. Whatever you say...Liz/Jim.

#1:   *(Just shakes, his/her head.)* **Look, Frank's/Jane's jacket is on the back of the chair. Put it on.**
(#2 puts on the jacket.)

#1:   **Clip the microphone here.** *(Pause)* **So, you ready?**

#2:   **You bet! Let's do it!**

#1:   *(To the booth)* **How are we doing? Is it about time?** *(Off-stage: Ten seconds.)* **Remember. When that little light goes on, we're on the air.** *(Off-stage: And in 5, 4, 3, 2, ...#1 Smiles.)* **Good evening. I'm Liz/Jim Nance.**

#2:   *(Horrified)* **And...I'm...Lisa/Larry.**
(#2 faints dead away and falls off camera. #1 watches, then looks back into the camera.)

#1:   **Welcome to the six o'clock news.**

16. The Order

(In a restaurant. #1 is at a table looking over the menu. #2, the waiter/waitress, comes over. #2 doesn't really pay much attention to #1.)

#2: Have you decided what you want?

#1: Not really. I'd like to know...

#2: Fine, what'll it be?

#1: I'm not sure. I was about to say I'd like to hear about your specials.

#2: Why?

#1: Why? Because I might like to have one?

#2: And you want me to explain them?

#1: Well, since I don't know what they are and you're the only one at this table who does, by process of elimination...

#2: I get it. The specials today are... *(Checks his/her pad)* ...fish and meat.

#1: Fish and meat?

#2: You need that defined?

#1: No, I've got a grasp of the basics, but you might want to fill me in on some of the details.

#2: Like what?

#1: Oh, I don't know. Maybe what kind of fish or what kind of meat.

#2: My, but you just want the moon, don't you? OK, we have... *(Checks his/her pad again)* ...white fish, and red meat. Happy?

#1: *(Hands #2 his/her menu.)* Ecstatic. Know what, just bring me a Chinese Chicken salad, please.

#2: If you wanted a Chinese Chicken Salad, why did you ask me about the specials?

#1: I don't know. I guess deep down I'm just evil.

69

#2: *(To himself/herself)* You won't get an argument from me. *(To #1)* Fine, Chicken Salad it is. *(Exits.)*

#1: *(Pulls out a small tape recorder. Turns it on and speaks into it.)* Note to myself: don't eat at this restaurant anymore. Now, notes on patient Jane Bryant. After our last session it's apparent that Jane's anxiety stems from a deep-seated...

#2: *(Come back to the table, waits.)* Ahem. Do you think you can tear yourself away from your little recorder?

#1: *(Turns back and sees #2.)* I'm sorry. I didn't see you.

#2: Of course you didn't. Why would you? I'm just the waiter/waitress. I'm sure you have much more important people to deal with.

#1: What can I do for you?

#2: We're all out of chicken. You can have a Chinese salad.

#1: There's no such thing as a Chinese salad.

#2: There is today.

#1: Just bring me a club sandwich. *(#2 doesn't move.)*

#1: What?

#2: You might try please. "Bring me a club sandwich, please." I'm your waiter/waitress, not your slave.

#1: OK, that's enough. Outside of existing and breathing, have I done something to offend you?

#2: What are you talking about?

#1: Since you first came over here, you've been curt, sarcastic, and rude. If you were a French waiter/waitress, I'd expect it. But since you're not, it's obvious you're very angry about something and you're taking it out on me.

#2: Thanks for the analysis. And what are you? A shrink?

#1: Actually...I am a therapist.

#2: Terrific. Seventy-five tables here and I have to wait on Sigmund Freud.

#1: That's enough. I want to talk to your manager.

#2: Sure, talk to the manager. Get me fired. Prove to him/her that he/she is right.

#1: Prove to who, what?

#2:   My wife/husband. He/she said this was a dead end job and I was a loser. You getting me fired should prove that.

#1:   Your wife/husband said you were a loser?

#2:   Can you believe that? He/she never used to say that. Especially when I was working and putting her/him through podiatry school?

#1:   Your husband/wife is a podiatrist?

#2:   Yes he/she is. Why? Is something wrong with that? You have something against feet?

#1:   No, not at all...I love feet. I use mine...every day. They're very...handy. Get it? Feet...hand... *(Pause)* It was a joke.

#2:   Really. I hope you're a better therapist than you are a comedian.

#1:   Do you know you're very hostile?

#2:   Sigmund Freud and Dick Tracy. What gave it away?

#1:   Fine. Vent away, but you're targeting your anger at the wrong person.

#2:   Maybe, but you're here, so that makes it at least convenient.

#1:   Not to mention counter-productive.

#2:   What does that mean?

#1:   Think about it. You're upset at your wife/husband. But instead of dealing with him/her, you're venting your anger at everyone except him/her. Now, what if some one does talk to your manager and you get fired? You said it yourself. You will prove your wife/husband right. And it won't be because your are a loser, but because you're allowing yourself to become a loser. It's simply a matter of self-loathing.

      (There is a pause.)

#2:   You wanna say that in English?

#1:   Bottom line, you don't like yourself. Period!

#2:   *(Sits at the table.)* What am I suppose to do?

#1:   *(Looks around.)* Don't you have other tables to wait on? Other customers to abuse?

#2:   Forget them! What can I do?

#1:   OK, answer this, do you like being a waiter?

#2:   Yes. I love it.

#1:   Good. Aside from today, are you a good waiter and do you make a decent living?

#2:   I'm great at it and I can make a lot of money.

#1:   Then answer me this, if what you said is the truth, how can you be a loser and this be a dead end job?

#2:   *(Pause)* You're right. *(Gets up and his/her voice starts to rise.)* I'm a great waiter/waitress. In fact, I'm one of the best in town and anyone who disagrees can just come here, get a table, sit down, order, and watch me! *(#1 and #2 look around.)*

#1:   That's great, but you may want to keep this between us right now.

#2:   OK, you're right, but how do I prove this to my wife/husband?

#1:   What have we been talking about? You only have to prove it to yourself. Want to know how?

#2:   Yes!

#1:   Great. Take all that anger and put it in your locker with your jacket and take it home to your husband/wife. Then be just what you said you were, the best waiter/waitress in the city. Hey, let's start now. Say to me, "Hi there. How are you? Nice day, isn't it?" *(Pause)* Well, go ahead.

#2:   Oh, OK. Hi there. How are you? Nice day, isn't it?

#1:   Great. Yes, it's a great day. Now ask me what I'd like. Go ahead.

#2:   What can I get for you, sir? Can I tell you about the specials? See, I remembered that you asked me about the specials before.

#1:   You are good. No, no specials, but I would love a club sandwich on toast. Now say, "It would be my pleasure" and go get it for me.

#2:   Sir, it would be my pleasure. I'll have it for you in a flash. I threw that in.

#1:   Nice touch. Now, go get it!

#2:   Now, go get it!

#1:   No, don't repeat it. Do it!

#2:   Oh. You bet!

      (#2 exits. #1 watches him/her go.)

#1:   *(Pause)* It's getting harder and harder just to order lunch in this town. *(Picks up the recorder again.)* Back to Jane Bryant. Her problems seem to stem from self- loathing... wait, that's the waiter/waitress...

17. The Package

(At a dock warehouse. It is the customs service warehouse. #1, a customs agent, is behind a counter. #2 walks up to the counter. #1 barely looks up.)

#1: May I help you?

#2: I hope so. I've been wandering around this place for an hour. Am I at the right station?

#1: That depends. Are you supposed to be here?

#2: That's what I'm trying to find out.

#1: Have you a bill of lading?

#2: A what?

#1: A bill of lading.

#2: I have no idea. This is what I was sent. *(Hands #1 an invoice. #1 takes a look at it.)* Is that a bill of lading?

#1: No.

#2: *(Pause)* Well, what is it?

#1: It's a request for clarification. *(Hands the paper back to #2.)*

#2: OK. What needs to be clarified and am I in the right place for that? *(#1 takes the paper again, looks at it, reaches under the counter, pulls out a storage box, and places it on the counter.)*

#1: This and yes.

#2: What is that?

#1: It's the contents of a package addressed to you from one, *(Reads)* Vladimir Borzov, of what was the former Soviet Union.

#2: Wait, are you saying you opened my package?

#1: We're the government. We can do that.

#2: But it's a federal offense to tamper with the U.S. mail.

#1: First, it started out as Russian mail, before it became U.S. mail. U.S. mail and U.S. Government both start with U.S. which stands for "us."

74

#2: No...it stands for United States.

#1: Which is who we are. We're the government. We do what we want.

#2: I see. So...why did you open my package from my Uncle Vlad?

#1: So you do acknowledge kinship with this Valdimir Borzov.

#2: "Acknowledge kinship"? Who talks like that?

#1: We're the government. We do.

#2: OK. Yes, Vladimir Borzov is my relative. My grandfather's uncle.

#1: So, he's actually your great-uncle.

#2: I don't know how great he is, but he's always been pretty good. *(Chuckles a bit. #1 has no reaction.)* Don't tell me, you have no sense of humor. You're the government.

#1: Exactly right.

#2: It's going to be a long day.

#1: It very well could be if you don't explain yourself sufficiently.

#2: What's to explain? I got a package from a relative in Russia.

#1: Correction, you received a Communist package from a Communist relative.

#2: A Communist package? Unless you've had your head buried in the sand...or somewhere else, the Cold War is over. There are no more Communists.

#1: That's what they'd like you to think.

#2: Really, it's the truth. It was in all the papers.

#1: We know. You read what we want you to read. It's our job to look out for you.

#2: Then how come there's no national health care plan?

#1: Because that would take free enterprise away from the insurance companies. If free enterprise goes, so does the democratic way of life. If that happens, know what we get?

#2: Communism?

#1: Didn't take two guesses, did it...Comrade?

#2: Never mind. Can I just have my package, please?

#1: I told you, not until you explain some of the items this Communist sent you.

#2: My uncle Vlad is not a Communist, he's a baker. Besides, he's sent me things before.

#1: But never things like these! *(Reaches into the box and pulls out a Russian flag.)* Care to explain this?

#2: It's an old Russian flag.

#1: And what do you plan to do with it?

#2: *(Pause)* Make a jacket out of it. I plan on holding on to it. It's a collector's item.

#1: And what kind of sicko would collect this?

#2: Historians, colleges, museums. You know, real subversives.

#1: Then what about this? *(Pulls out a small doll.)*

#2: It's an ordinary doll. It was probably intended for my daughter.

#1: It looks ordinary. So did a particular box of Jello until they found some microfilm hidden in it.

#2: If you're referring to the atom bomb spies, the microfilm was in a fake hollow coin. Two halves of a Jello box were used as a signal.

#1: Know your spy history pretty well, don't you!?

#2: OK, that's it! I've received things from my uncle before and I have never gone through this. I'd like to see an order authorizing you to do this to me.

#1: No, we're the...

#2: Don't even think of saying that. If you're truly the government you thrive on paper. It's probably there in triplicate. Show it to me! *(#1 reluctantly hands #2 a piece of paper. #2 starts to get very angry.)* I wasn't sent a clarification notice. This says I have to pay twenty-five dollars duty on these items and that it will be collected here by a trainee customs agent.

#1:   I...I wouldn't believe everything you read.

#2:   On every piece of garbage I'm told. What are you trying to do to me?

#1:   You're a Communist sympathizer and I seem to be the only one around here who realizes that. I may just be a trainee right now, but I can spot a Communist a mile away. Soon they'll all find out I'm right, and when they do...I'll be a hero!

#2:   You know, I'd like to stay here and debate this with you, but I'm due back on the planet Earth very soon. So, here's what we're going to do.

#1:   No, wait...

#2:   No, you wait! Don't talk, just listen! I am going to take my box of harmless presents from my foreign uncle and leave. You − are going to pay the duty on this package yourself.

#1:   And why would I do that?

#2:   Because if you don't, I am going to sue your red, white, and blue behind, the U.S. Customs Service, and anyone else who might have had a hand in hiring a deranged Joe McCarthy throwback who doesn't realize that it's not 1951!

#1:   You can't do that.

#2:   Correction, I'm a U.S. citizen. I can sue anyone I want. *(Picks up his/her box and walks away.)*

#1:   *(Pulls out a pad and pen.)* I have to remember that one. "I'm a U.S. citizen..."

18. The Platter

(In the manager's office of a very expensive store. #1, a customer, is waiting. #2, the manager, enters.)

#2: **Good afternoon. I'm Mr./Ms. Upson.** *(Sits down at the desk.)* **What can I do for you?**

#1: **I bought this...** *(Holds up a platter.)*

#2: *(Notices something on the monitor sitting on his/her desk.)* **Yes, I'm sure you have a fascinating story, but I have to take care of something important at this moment. Excuse me.** *(Dials the phone.)* **Walters, Upson here. I'm sitting at my desk looking at my monitor and guess what I see?** *(Pause)* **No, you'd like to think that I see an orderly store, but look over in the watch section. Please tell me that it's just my imagination and you didn't allow that Madonna person in here to shop again.** *(Pause)* **I don't care. You let her in, you ask her to leave. Do it now!** *(Hangs up.)*

#1: **I didn't mean to eavesdrop, but are you throwing out Madonna? The Madonna?**

#2: **There was another, but she died several millennia ago? So I am referring to the...for lack of a better description, the singer.**

#1: **What did she do?**

#2: **Nothing. We allow some of those show business people to shop here, but she...well, she shows a little too much skin for our taste**

#1: **Boy, you all are strict.**

#2: **Yes, we are. Now, what seems to be your problem?**

#1: **I bought this platter here for my parents' anniversary. You said you'd engrave it and send it to me when it was done.**

#2: **Since you have it with you, I'm assuming we did that.**

#1: **Yes, you did.**

#2: So you're here to congratulate us on a job well done?

#1: Not exactly. You made a mistake when you engraved it.

#2: I doubt that. Let me see the platter. *(#1 hands #2 the platter.) (#2 looks it over.)* It looks fine to me. I see no problem.

#1: You're joking, right? Did you read it?

#2: Of course I did.

#1: *(Takes the platter back and reads it.)* Let me get this straight, you find nothing wrong with, "March 30. Happy Anniversary, MOP and Pop?"

#2: No, I don't.

#1: *(Pause)* Is English your native language? Who calls their mother Mop?!

#2: Let me ask you something. Do you know what's just outside our front door?

#1: Rodeo Drive.

#2: Exactly. That means that we are quite exclusive and cater to what can be a very diverse and sometimes unusual clientele. The nicknames these people have for their parents run the gamut from A-Z and then some. There was even one man who referred to his mother as his "cuddle-buddy." A name reeking with Freudian overtones. You yourself refer to your father as "Pop." If I'm not mistaken, a "pop" is a carbonated beverage, not a parental figure.

#1: A lot of people refer to their fathers as "Pop."

#2: Perhaps, so maybe some people do refer to their mothers as "Mop", n'est pas?

#1: Fine, I'll give you that point.

#2: Of course you will.

#1: But I don't call my mother "Mop." Face it, your engraver made a mistake.

#2: Assuming that's true, what do you want from me?

#1: What do I want?

#2: Is that a tough question? Should I use smaller words?

#1: No, it's not a tough question. It is however, ridiculous.

What I want is for you to fix it! I want you to change it to read "Mom and Pop."

#2: Fine, what do you suggest? Should we use a big eraser or perhaps try some whiteout.

#1: I'm not following you.

#2: As if you could. *(Holds up the platter.)* This is platinum. The names are etched in. We can't just change them.

#1: Then get me a new platter.

#2: That leads us to problem number two. This platter was a sale item.

#1: Sale?! That platter cost me a thousand dollars.

#2: Like I said, a sale item. *(Shows #1 his/her watch.)* See this watch? The minute hand costs a thousand dollars. We offered these platters for sale until we realized no one with taste would buy them. So we lowered the price and if I'm not mistaken, you got the last.

#1: So you're saying you won't replace it?

#2: Finally, a spark of understanding.

#1: What am I supposed to do about the inscription?

#2: Well, since this is a serving platter, maybe if you cover the inscription with food, no one will notice.

#1: You're not helping.

#2: OK, just so you won't think that I'm the cold, caustic, unfeeling store manager that I actually am, I'm going to make an exchange for you. *(Reaches into a desk drawer and pulls out a little box and opens it.)* I will exchange your platter for these.

#1: What are they?

#2: Solid gold toothpicks. They were a novelty item several years ago. They actually sell for $600 dollars apiece, but I'll make it a straight trade.

#1: You expect me to give my parents toothpicks for their anniversary?!

#2: Why not? If you're a typical example of your family's lineage, I'm sure your parents would enjoy a good pick when they finish their vittles.

#1: That should just about do it. Look, you can keep the toothpicks. I've decided to give my parents something much better for their anniversary.

#2: And what is that?

#1: You.

#2: I'm sorry, I don't understand.

#1: Of course you don't. I'll explain and go slowly so you can get every word. My parents have their own very successful law firm. My mother is also a consumer advocate and handles many cases in that area. You remember that "exclusive" clothing store, I believe it was just up the block from here, that refused to wait on a woman they saw as the "wrong kind" for the store.

#2: Yes.

#1: Well, my mother was that woman's attorney and, let's put it this way, that "wrong kind" of woman — now owns that store.

#2: That was...your mother?

#1: Old "Mop" herself. And I'm going to hand her this store and you on a badly engraved platter.

#2: I don't think...

#1: Well, maybe you should because by the time my mother's done, I will get satisfaction and the next thing you say to a customer will probably be "Would you like fries with that?"

#2: You know sir/ma'am, there's no real reason to bother your mother. I just remembered that we do have another platter we can get. It's a little more expensive $5000...

#1: I'm not paying any more.

#2: No, of course you're not. It'll be a...straight trade. I'll... even get it engraved. Correctly.

#1: Of course you will. I'd appreciate that. My address is on the sales slip. Have it sent over by five – the latest.

#2: Certainly.

#1: Thank you. *(Starts to exit, then comes back to #2.)* **You**

know, I've got something stuck in my tooth. You wouldn't happen to have a toothpick, would you? *(#2 holds up the box with the gold toothpicks, takes one and puts it in his/her mouth.)* Today turned out to be a pretty good day after all, don't you think? Bye.

19. The Roommate

(In a living room. #1 enters. He/she has come home from a long day's work. #1 looks around. The apartment is a mess. #1 puts his/her things down and starts to straighten a little. #2 enters.)

#2: I thought I heard someone out here.

#1: Is it too much to ask for you to straighten this place up?

#2: I did.

#1: You call this straight?

#2: Yes. You should have seen it this morning.

#1: And what did that look like?

#2: I could tell you, but then I'd have to kill you. *(No response.)* Well, someone's in a bad mood. What happened? You miss your visit from the Happy Elf today?

#1: No, I'm just tired of sharing an apartment with a pig.

#2: I'm not a pig. I'm messy. There's a difference.

#1: Sorry. I didn't know that filth came in gradations.

#2: See, pigs are dirty and unclean. I'm not. I'm just not tidy.

#1: Well, keep trying. I'm sure you'll hit the top of the grunge scale before too long.

#2: What is your problem?

#1: *(Sits on the couch.)* I've had a long day at work and all I wanted to do was come home and unwind.

#2: So...unwind.

#1: Where? The apartment is full of...you and your debris. *(Lifts a blanket off a pile of newspapers on the couch.)* Like this! Don't you think you can get rid of some of these?

#2: No. I haven't read them all yet. I don't want to miss what's going on.

#1: They've been lying around here forever.

#2: They have not.

#1: *(Takes a paper from the pile.)* Really? *(Reads the paper.)* "Allies Invade Normandy"? *(Lifting up another paper)* **Or**

83

this one, "Titanic Sinks!"

#2: Fine! I'll move the newspapers into my room.

#1: And that's another thing. Since when is it "your room"? It's my guest room.

#2: Being a bit possessive, aren't we?

#1: No, it's just that when one pays the rent, when one pays the utilities, when one pays the phone, that one usually has the right to claim ownership. I'm making that claim.

#2: Hey, I've put in for things.

#1: Excuse me, but seven pieces of paper that say, "IOU for electricity and stuff" hardly constitutes any payment.

#2: What does it constitute?

#1: Freeloading.

#2: Well, thank you very much. At least I know where I stand. You know, you seem to be forgetting about all that food I bought last week.

#1: True. Then you had a party and you and your friends ate it all.

#2: Hey, you could have come. You were invited.

#1: How thoughtful of you to invite me to a party in my own home. Your generosity obviously knows no bounds.

#2: Am I still sensing a little hostility coming from your direction?

#1: And people say you're slow to catch on.

#2: If you have something to say, just say it! It's very cleansing. I won't mind.

#1: *(Walks up to #2.)* Good! You are an incredibly annoying twit!

#2: *(Pause)* My, that was blunt, wasn't it?

#1: I know things have been rough since your breakup, but you were not supposed to be a permanent fixture in my house.

#2: "Permanent fixture"? You make me sound like the garbage disposal.

#1: *(Pause, then to him/herself)* No, I can't. It's too easy. *(To #2)* I thought you were just going to stay here until you got back on your feet.

#2: Do I appear to be back on my feet?

#1: Who can tell? There's rarely a time you're ever off the couch. I don't even know if your feet still work.

#2: I'd be careful if I were you. The time right after a messy divorce is the most crucial. Psychologically speaking, that is. Any more pressure, from anywhere, could push me right over the edge.

#1: The edge of what?!

#2: My mental stability.

#1: You're assuming you had any stability to begin with. And what is all this "messy divorce"? Your marriage was annulled. You two were together less than ten weeks. Hey, you've been here longer than that.

#2: Exactly, and now I'm just starting to put down some roots and you want to yank them out.

#1: Don't even think of planting anything here. This is my house, not the north forty, and you are a guest who has long overstayed his/her welcome.

#2: Are you kicking me out?

#1: No, friends wouldn't do that. I'm...suggesting that it might be time for you to move on. Get your life together, figure out what you want to do, meet new people, go places, do things and GET OUT!

#2: See, I don't think I should leave when you're in such an agitated state.

#1: *(Jumps at #2.)* Who do you think put me in this state? *(#2 backs away from #1. They start circling the couch.)*

#2: Maybe you should try and stay calm.

#1: Oh, I am calm. As a matter of fact, the prosecution will probably remark to the jury how calm I was when I took your life and the glee I had admitting to it.

#2: Violence is never the answer, you know.

#1: Unless the question is how do you get rid of a pain in the butt.

(There is a slight run around the couch and #2 finally stops.)

#2: **Look, this is stupid...not to mention tiring. Let's just be adults.**

#1: **You want to be adults? Fine! You have thirty minutes to gather as much of your...stuff as you can and get out!**

#2: **But...**

#1: **No buts. And if you're not out of here, and soon, I'm going to the garage to get my weed wacker.**

#2: *(Pause)* **What does that mean?**

#1: **I'm not sure, but it sounds real ugly, doesn't it? Are you going?** *(Lunges at #2.)*

#2: **Yes, I'm going!** *(Pause)* **Maybe you're right. I'll get my things and be out in an hour.** *(#1 starts to say something.)* **I mean, half an hour.** *(Starts to exit, stops and turns back.)* **Just one more thing. Can I borrow your car? Mine's in the shop...** *(#1 takes off after #2 and they both exit.)*

20. The Script

(In a restaurant. #1 is at a table. He/she is a film producer. A very important person — especially in his or her own mind. #1 is on a cellular phone.)

#1: No, I told you I was very busy. *(Pause)* You don't believe me? Well how's this. I had to make an appointment three weeks in advance with myself just to have lunch today. So I really don't have the time to waste talking to you. Get it? *(Pause)* If I want to talk to you, I'll call! OK!? *(Pause)* Fine! Good-bye, mom. *(Hangs up the phone.)* Some people!

#2: *(Comes rushing over to the table and sits down.)* I am so sorry that I am late, but you know what traffic is like this time of day. I would have called, but I don't have your cellular number. So I just came right over. I know how important this meeting is. *(Looks out over the restaurant.)* Waiter, could you bring me a mineral water. Thanks. *(Turns back to #1.)* So, should we start the meeting?

#1: *(Staring at #2)* Who are you?!

#2: Your lunch meeting.

#1: I don't have a lunch meeting.

#2: Well, officially - no, but I knew you were going to be here, so I figured why waste an hour.

#1: Very considerate. *(Pause)* Who are you?!

#2: I'm a blessing from heaven.

#1: *(Stands.)* I'm going to have you removed! Waiter!

#2: *(Pulls #1 back into his/her chair.)* Wait! You don't want to do that. You and I may never get this chance again.

#1: Really? That's too bad. Hopefully God will be merciful when he judges me. Waiter!

(#1 stands and #2 pulls him/her down again.)

#2: I know what it is — you're hungry. Why don't we order first. Then we can talk business. *(Picks up a menu and* *opens it.)* **So, what looks good?**

#1: **You – deceased.**

#2: **Hey, that's funny. No, seriously, what do you want?**

#1: **You to evaporate.**

#2: **Sorry, can't do that. Not just yet.**

#1: **Let me ask you something. Are you my punishment for some past life transgression?**

#2: **Actually, I'm your savior. I'm here to save you.**

#1: **From what?**

#2: **From yourself. From your mediocre existence.**

#1: **Excuse me, but I am not in any way, shape, or form mediocre.**

#2: **Let me rephrase; no, you personally are not mediocre. You are one of Hollywood's biggest producers, but the product you give us...well...**

#1: **I'll have you know my last three movies have grossed at least 200 million apiece. I'm a deity in this town.**

#2: **Hey, if you want to judge success on money, that's your business. I'm talking about raising your sense of values. Lifting your artistic standards to a new level. I can do that for you.**

#1: **Oh no! I've got it. You're an actor, right?**

#2: **Don't be ridiculous.**

#1: **Then you must be worse. But what's worse than an actor?** *(Pause)* **OH-MY-GOD! You're a writer!**
   (#2 just smiles at #1. #1 backs away from #2.)

#2: **Relax, I'm harmless.**

#1: **Writers are never harmless. I'm surprised you're here alone. Don't you people usually travel in packs?**

#2: **Not always.**

#1: **And if you're here, I'm sure there's some over-written, voluminous, collection of scrap paper you like to refer to as a script lurking somewhere in the vicinity.**

#2: **Funny you should say that.** *(Brings out a phone-book sized script and drops it on the table.)*

#1: What is that?!

#2: Your escape from oblivion.

#1: That's not a script, it's a tome!

#2: It's a masterpiece. I want you to know that I've been working on this for almost a month. I'm very serious about it.

#1: How long is that...that...thing?

#2: Page-wise – I'm not sure. But I figure that in this form, the movie should run about nine hours.

#1: Nine hours!? Are you insane!? Nobody's going to sit through a nine hour movie!

#2: Sure they will. Don't sell the public short. They sat through "Dances With Wolves," didn't they?

#1: "Dances With Wolves" was three hours long.

#2: Really? Hmm. Seemed like nine. Anyway, enough on that piece of garbage. This is the baby that's going to make you a hit in this town.

#1: *(Jumps up.)* I'M ALREADY A HIT IN THIS TOWN!

#2: Just in your own mind. Look, why don't you sit down.

#1: Because obviously you are a lunatic who escaped from some asylum.

#2: No, Orange County.

#1: Same thing. What will it take to make you go away?

#2: Listen to me. Seriously.

#1: *(Pause)* If there's the slightest chance you'll go...I'll listen. *(Sits back down.)* So, regale me with your literary prowess.

#2: What?

#1: Read!

#2: Oh. Well, this is a great story that's full of everything.

#1: Of that I'm sure.

#2: I like to see it as a cross between "Home Alone" and "Platoon."

#1: You're joking?!

#2: Not at all. It's the story of a little boy whose father is

going off to Vietnam and the boy sneaks off to Nam with
his dad by hiding in his duffel bag.

#1: *(Pause)* I'm speechless.

#2: I knew you would be. Anyway, the father's jeep is
ambushed and everyone is killed...

#1: Except the little boy.

#2: Of course. He's left alone in Hanoi and to avenge his
father's death, he becomes the youngest, smallest special
forces officer in history.

#1: And he single-handedly wins the war, right?

#2: Yes...or he steps on a land mine and blows up. I haven't
decided yet. I have two endings.

#1: And what do you plan to call this epic you're going to
inflict on the public?

#2: "A Connecticut Child in Ho Chi Min's Court."

#1: That does it. OK, I have now listened to you and your
asinine idea. Now before I have you taken into the
kitchen and boiled, run, do not walk, to the nearest exit
and take your pitiful scribblings with you.

#2: But...

#1: GO!

#2: You know, you try and do some people a favor and they
can't see a good thing when it's staring them in the face.
Suit yourself! Enjoy your mediocrity.
*(#2 marches off in a huff. #1 watches him/her go, then picks
up his/her cellular phone and dials.)*

#1: Murray *(Pause)* shut up and listen. I want you to stop
production on that space thing we're doing. *(Pause)* Why?
I'll tell you why. I just got a brilliant idea for a new film.
It takes place in Vietnam...

21. The Show

*(In a studio. There is preparation going on for the show "A.M. —
THIS MORNING.")*

ALLEN: *(Voice Off-stage)* **Let's settle everyone. We're on in ten
seconds. Camera one, get the sign. Camera two – get
the set. And in five...four...three...two...**
(We come up from black on the sign.)
(MUSIC) (Voice Off-stage) **"Good morning and
welcome to A.M. This Morning with your hosts, Chris
Barnes and Kerry Foster.**

CHRIS: **Good morning. We have a great show for you today.
In a moment we're going to take you to my interview
with the Vice-President of the United States where
we talked about the growing health care problem in
the country.**

KERRY: **And after that, I'm going to take you to the zoo
where Foo-Foo the elephant gave birth to a new baby
yesterday.**

CHRIS: **Sounds like fun, Kerry. So if you'll all sit back, have
your coffee, we'll be back right after these
messages.**
(They both sit back and smile.)

ALLEN: *(Voice Off-stage)* **And we're clear.**

KERRY: **That's it! I have had it!**

CHRIS: **Oh, no! Not again.**

KERRY: **Allen! Allen, get down here. We've got to talk!**

ALLEN: *(Voice Off-stage)* **Forget it, Kerry. Why don't you just
call your agent...again. Or talk to Robert. He's the
producer.**

KERRY: **Fine. Get him on the phone.**

CHRIS: **That might prove to be a little problematic.**

KERRY: **Why?**

91

CHRIS: Because at this precise moment he's in the Bahamas at the bottom of the ocean.

KERRY: Visiting relatives, no doubt.

CHRIS: Scuba diving.

KERRY: So? That little maggot doesn't go anywhere without his cellular phone. I'm sure he's had it waterproofed. Somebody call him!

CHRIS: What is your problem?

KERRY: What's my problem!? That should be obvious even to a moron like you. You get the V.P., I get Foo-Foo. You talk to the Pope, I get Popeye. See a pattern?

CHRIS: You're just blowing it out of proportion. You get a lot of good stories.

KERRY: Really? Name one.

CHRIS: How about that 105 year old woman you interviewed.

KERRY: Yeah, great story. You know what her hobby was? Knitting slipcovers for her dead friend's coffins.

CHRIS: That aside, she was very sweet.

KERRY: She was in a home! She also thought I was Edward R. Murrow. She kept asking how the war was going in Europe.

CHRIS: So what do you want?

KERRY: To practice journalism. I want to have the same chances you do.

CHRIS: But we're different people.

KERRY: No kidding! I've got a Masters in journalism from Yale and you went...where? The Columbus School of Broadcasting, wasn't it?

CHRIS: Wait a minute...

KERRY: Hey, don't get me wrong. I'm sure it was a very good school. I like how they put your name on your diploma with stick-on letters.

CHRIS: Are you finished?

KERRY: I haven't even started. I'm tired of lousy stories, an awful director, inept assistants, imbecilic writers...

CHRIS: Gee, I can't imagine why no one wants to cooperate with you.

KERRY: Why, because I'm honest?

CHRIS: No, I think there's a better term for you.

KERRY: And that is?

CHRIS: You're...a jerk.

KERRY: I beg your pardon.

CHRIS: You're mean. Nobody likes you.

KERRY: That's not true.

CHRIS: You went to Yale and can't see the plain facts.

KERRY: What facts?

CHRIS: You've just called various members of our staff, maggots, terrible, imbeciles, and inept. You called me a moron. Am I leaving anything out?

KERRY: Yeah, you've got bad hair, too.

CHRIS: You know, you can pontificate all you want about your education and degrees but I'll always have something that you never will.

KERRY: What?

CHRIS: A T-V-Q. People turn on the set, and they like me. They tolerate you. You're basically necessary, but irrelevant.

KERRY: Who do you think you're talking to?

CHRIS: I know exactly. My sidekick.

KERRY: Your sidekick?

CHRIS: Hey, just accept it. You're my Ed McMahon, my...Miss Piggy.

KERRY: Oh, you're treading a real thin line here, Pal.

CHRIS: No, I'm not. I just understand what kind of show we've got.

KERRY: And you think it's a good news show?

CHRIS: I don't think it's a news show at all. Nothing we report is current — and you know what, that's just fine with me.

KERRY: Boy, you are some reporter. Now I really know where

you studied journalism...Sears!

CHRIS: When are you going to wake up and smell the Perrier. This is Hollywood. We're a morning show. How many serious news shows do you know that start at 7:10? All the good ones at least start on the half hour.

KERRY: And you're content to just let it remain that way?

CHRIS: You bet!

KERRY: You are so, spineless. You're pathetic, you're a fake, you're...

CHRIS: Very rich. Hey, I could do this show in my sleep...

KERRY: I always assumed you did.

CHRIS: Whatever. It's a no brainer. Besides, where else could I make $400,000 a year?

KERRY: You make $400,000?! For that!?

CHRIS: Staggers the imagination, doesn't it?

KERRY: That's not fair. I make...

CHRIS: A lot less! And whose fault is that? The survey says... "yours." We've got a top rated show, so your job is safe, BUT...you're under contract for another three years and as long as you remain a pain in... well, things will never change.

KERRY: That stinks!

CHRIS: I couldn't agree more. The best thing you could do for yourself is shut up, pucker up and well – you know the rest.

KERRY: OK, you listen to me – you all listen to me...

ALLEN: *(Off-stage)* Uh, Kerry...

KERRY: Shut up, Allen! You listen, too.

ALLEN : OK. We're all listening.

KERRY: Maybe I am locked into this turkey for another three years, but things are going to change, otherwise it will be three years of hell! And, partner, you can take your advice, stick it, then you pucker up.

(Silence.)

94

ALLEN: *(Off-stage)* **Kerry?**

KERRY: **What do you want, Allen!?**

ALLEN: **We're on the air.**

KERRY: *(Turns to the camera, looks in and changes to a smile.)* **Hi, welcome back to the show...**

22. The Shrink

(The lunch room / lounge of a large magazine. #1, a psychologist, is there. #2 enters.)

#1: Mr./Ms. Watkins? Please sit down. I'm Dr. Schneck.

#2: *(Sits.)* I'm sorry, did you say Schneck?

#1: Yes.

#2: Wow. You know, for fifty bucks, I can put you in touch with a guy that can take care of the people who gave you that name.

#1: I'll have you know that Schneck is a very old family name. It is of German derivation and dates back several centuries.

#2: I see. So you're proud to come from a long line of Bavarian Schnecks.

#1: I...I suppose one might put it that way.

#2: No supposing necessary. I just did. But to each his own. So Schnecky, what can I do for you?

#1: It's Dr. Schnecky...uh Schneck and you can take this meeting a little more seriously.

#2: Fine, I'll be as serious as a heart attack — as soon as you tell me why I'm here.

#1: I haven't told you?

#2: No. Having a short term memory problem, Doc?

#1: No, I've just seen so many people in the last couple of days that I guess I'm a little...little...uhh...

#2: Never mind. I get a little...uhh, myself on occasion. So, what's up?

#1: I'm a psychologist and I was hired by your boss, Mr. Wapple, to try and find out why morale has been so low here at the magazine.

#2: That's easy, I can tell you why right now.

#1: What is it?

#2:   You've taken over the lunch room. We get very cranky when we have no place to eat.

#1:   I think Mr. Wapple feels that this morale problem started before I got here. Now, Mr./Ms. Watkins...

#2:   Please, call me Tommy/Tammy.

#1:   *(Checks his/her file.)* But you're name is Dean/Deena.

#2:   I know.

#1:   Then why do you want me to call you Tommy/Tammy?

#2:   I've always liked that name. I was curious to hear how it would sound.

#1:   *(Slams the file shut.)* Mr./Ms. Watkins! You're not being very cooperative. Why is that?

#2:   I don't know. You're the shrink. You tell me.

#1:   Maybe you think this whole thing is foolish?

#2:   BINGO! Right on the money! Can I go now?

#1:   No! Mr. Wapple doesn't share that opinion.

#2:   And which Mr. Wapple is that? Junior or senior?

#1:   Junior.

#2:   Figures. He's probably just upset about the suggestion box.

#1:   Aha! So you do know about that!

#2:   Aha! Who doesn't? He sent around a memo asking people to start putting real suggestions in the box.

#1:   Do you know what was in there?

#2:   I've heard stories.

#1:   Let me read you some. *(Takes out some notes and starts to read them.)* "I think we should start using elves as reporters. They're little and can get into places that big reporters can't. They also like to work at night and we can pay them less." *(Takes out another one.)* Or this one, "How about if we write all our articles in Sanskrit?" Or this one...well, this one suggests Mr. Wapple put his head somewhere that's physically impossible. These are just a few of the hundred or so that have been in the box. Mr. Wapple just wants to know who's doing this and why.

#2:   And how do you plan to find out?

#1: By giving everyone a few simple tests. Then I analyze their responses and that should tell me who is involved.

#2: What kind of tests are you talking about?

#1: Simple things like...word association, where...

#2: You say a word, then I say the first thing that comes to mind.

#1: Exactly! For example – I might say black and you would say...

#2: Affirmative action.

#1: What?

#2: Why.

#1: No.

#2: Yes.

#1: Stop!

#2: Go!

#1: Please!

#2: Thank you!

#1: Stop it! I'm not doing the test!

#2: *(Doesn't repeat.)* Oh. *(Pause)* Too bad. I was doing real well.

#1: No you weren't. When I said black you said affirmative action.

#2: We're doing a cover story on it and it's the first thing that came to mind. So according to the rules, it wasn't wrong. Boy, if you don't know that then you're not a very good shrink at all, are you?

#1: I happen to be an excellent shrink...uh, psychologist. Let's just move on to another test.

#2: You know what, I've got a better idea. Let's not!

#1: Are you refusing to take the tests?

#2: Yes.

#1: Why?

#2: We're not doing that word association thing again, are we?

#1: No.

#2: Good. Then I'll tell you why I don't want to take any tests. They're a waste of time. If you want to know if I know who wrote the suggestions, why don't you just...ask me?

#1: *(Eyes #2.)* Fine, I'll play your little game. Do you know who wrote the suggestions?

#2: Yes, I do. Ask me who it was.

#1: Who was it?

#2: Me. Now, ask me how many notes I wrote.

#1: How many did you write?

#2: All of them. Can you figure out what the next question should be?

#1: Why...did you write them?

#2: Very good. You're brighter than you appear. I wrote them because Wapple Jr. — sounds like a hamburger, doesn't it — anyway, he's an idiot.

#1: Actually, he happens to have a Ph.D. in...

#2: In business! He's trying to make this place like...a company. It's not. It's a magazine and he's talking to reporters and photographers, and ad people, and layout people. You can't talk to us like...normal people. We're a very quirky bunch. What he should do is either call a meeting and get to know us all, as we are, or just stick to the money end and stop trying to change things.

#1: Well why didn't you write that suggestion down and put it in the box?

#2: Simple — it wasn't funny. See you later, Doc. *(#2 gets up and starts to leave. He/she reaches into his/her pocket and pulls out one last note. #2 walks back to #1.)* Here you go. I wrote this suggestion for you when I was told to come here. *(Exits.)*

#1: *(Opens and reads the note.)* Oh my goodness! If I did that I'd be in therapy for years. I'd be...

23. The Sitcom

(In an office. #1 and #2 are writers. At present #1 is pacing and waiting for #2 to return. #1 finally goes to the phone, picks it up and dials.)

#1: Sally is he/she still in there? *(Pause)* I know, but it's only one script. It takes less time to read *War and Peace*! *(Just then #2 enters.)*

#2: Who are you talking to?

#1: Never mind, Sally. He's/She's here. *(#2 hangs the phone up.)* What took so long? I've been going crazy here.

#2: See, this is exactly why I don't let you go to these story meetings with me. You don't know how to stay calm.

#1: That's crap and you know it. I was calm for at least ...four minutes after you left.

#2: I rest my case.

#1: So, are you going to tell me what happened or not?

#2: Mitchell only liked half of our script.

#1: Which half?

#2: *(Takes a torn up script out of his/her bag.)* The top. *(Hands #1 the two halves of the script.)*

#1: I can't believe he ripped up our script.

#2: Actually, he wanted to burn it, but there are too many flammables in his office.

#1: Did he at least say exactly what didn't he like about it?

#2: Let's see, he hated the setting, the plot, the characters, the dialog, the...

#1: I get the picture. Was there anything he liked?

#2: The covers. He thought we picked out a nice color for the covers.

#1: Terrific. Well, this is just great. I knew something like this was going to happen. I told you we should have never tried to become producers. We should have just stayed staff writers.

#2: We couldn't. You got us fired, remember?

#1: Oh no. You can't blame that on me.

#2: I can't? Weren't you the one who called the star of the show a loud-mouth, classless cow, with no talent, whose number of writers is only exceeded by her number of husbands.

#1: Hey, a lot of people said those things about her.
(*#2 starts to say something, but #1 stops him/her.*) OK, I admit that I'm the only one who did it in a full page ad in *Variety*, but if you're going to do something, you might as well do it right.

#2: So it was your fault we got fired.

#1: Whatever...that's not relevant. What's important is what are we going to do now?!

#2: What we're not going to do is panic. There's nothing to worry about.

#1: Nothing to worry about? I know Mitchell's going to want us to come up with a new sitcom.

#2: He does and so we shall.

#1: When?

#2: (*Pause*) This afternoon.

#1: WHAT?! Are you crazy?! It took us a couple of weeks to come up with and write the last one.

#2: And that was our fatal mistake.

#1: What was?

#2: Taking our time to write an intelligent, quality show. Do you know the last time a show like that actually made it?

#1: 1968?

#2: '72, when *M*A*S*H* premiered. What we should have done was simply follow the "sitcom formula."

#1: What's the "sitcom formula"?

#2: It's the sure fire way to create a hit show.

#1:   Tell me about it.

#2:   As I understand it, what you need to do is find some basically talentless stand-up comic who's been on "The Tonight Show" once, surround him or her with supporting players that include at least one busty blonde, one weird guy or girl, an idiot, and a short or fat guy. Then, find some really stupid reason to connect them all together, steal an old episode of "I Love Lucy" to use as a pilot, and bingo, you've got yourself a hit.

#1:   And how do you know this will work?

#2:   Look at what's on T.V.

#1:   *(Pause)* Good point. OK, where do we start?

#2:   We need a no-talent comic.

#1:   Hey, how about that red-headed guy with the props?

#2:   Big Red!? He is bad. Perfect. Next we need a busty blonde.

#1:   Can't we just steal one from "Baywatch"? They have plenty.

#2:   Good idea. The other actors can be no-names who we don't have to pay a lot.

#1:   OK, so how do we connect them?

#2:   Easy, get the newspaper and start reading me story headlines.

#1:   *(Gets the paper and starts reading.)* "400 Pound Woman Eats Own Pet."

#2:   *(Pause)* It's got potential, but I think the SPCA will eventually get ticked off. Read me another.

#1:   "6 Inmates Escape Via Tunnel."

#2:   Wait! Stop! That's great. We cut it from six to four inmates and it'll be perfect.

#1:   Our stars are going to be criminals?

#2:   Sure,...but we'll make them...white collar criminals. No murderers or anything like that.

#1:   OK, then how about we say Big Red is this computer genius who got into the government's computer and gave money away to the poor.

#2: That's great. You've made him very sympathetic. OK so he's at this minimum security prison and he and three others tunnel out. Now, what's your favorite episode of "Lucy"?

#1: The one in Italy where she had to stomp on the grapes.

#2: *(Starts to think.)* Italy...vineyards...OK, how's this? The fat guy they escape with is Italian and has relatives in Italy who have this broken down old vineyard.

#1: And after they escape they sneak on a boat, take fake names, go to Italy, reopen the old winery, and hide out there making really bad wine.

#2: And not only will they be running from the American police, but trying to fool the Italians as well.

#1: This is great. And we get to use all those actors with all those funny little accents. This show will run forever.

#2: Forget forever, just hope it runs till we get syndication. OK, we've got to write this up. Get the pad.

#1: *(Goes to the desk and grabs a pad, then spots a Variety on the desk.)* Oh, no!

#2: What's wrong?

#1: Listen to what's in *Variety* this morning. "Big Red To Escape From Jail This Fall In New Show."

#2: Hey, I never said the "Sitcom Formula" was a secret. OK, so we just start over. What other comics do you know?

#1: There's that weird guy who was on Letterman last night.

#2: I saw him, too. You know, using him would kill two birds with one stone.

#1: And we could still steal the "Baywatch" blonde.

#2: Right. OK, read the paper.

#1: *(Picks up the paper and reads.)* "Guadalajara's Mayor Mounts a Moral Crusade."

#1/#2: MEXICO! Perfect!

24. The Soap Opera

(In a living room. #1 is on the phone.)

#1: You have no idea who you're talking to, do you? *(Pause)* Well, you should learn because anyone who knows me knows I won't tolerate that kind of threat. *(Pause)* What am I going to do? I'll put it very simply, if I don't get my money and get it by the end of the day, there's going to be help to fray and you can fake that to the tank!

#2: *(Off-stage)* **CUT!** *(We cut to #2 sitting in a chair next to a camera. Then back to #1 who slams down the phone.)*

#1: What are you cutting for? That was going great.

#2: *(Walks over to #1.)* Great? Great!? Jody, do you have any idea what you just said? Just the last two lines.

#1: Of course I do...let's see...I said, "there'll be help to fray and you can fake that to the tank."

#2: You're right, that's exactly what you said. So tell me *(Pause)* **WHAT DOES THAT MEAN!**

#1: **HOW SHOULD I KNOW?** I don't write this stuff, I just say what's in the script.

#2: No, no, if you said what was in the script, you would have said, "there'll be hell to pay and you can take that to the bank!"

#1: Oh. Well, you're right that does make a lot more sense.

#2: *(Tries to control himself/herself.)* Jody, when you get script changes right before we shoot, would you look at them with your glasses on? Please!

#1: I can't. You know how much I hate those things.

#2: We're not asking you to wear them on camera. Go in your dressing room, lock the door. No one will see you. Do it for the good of the show...please!

#1: Well...if it's for the good of the show...OK.

#2: *(Through clenched teeth)* **Thank you!** *(Pause)* **OK**

everyone, we'll pick up right here after lunch. That's one hour. *(Yells off the set)* And Joe, I don't mean an hour and a half. *(Starts to exit.)*

#1: Frank/Fran, before you go, we need to talk.

#2: Jody, it's not a good time and I am not in the mood.

#1: Well you better get in the mood. This is very important and it affects the whole show.

#2: *(Gives in.)* OK, Jody, what's so important?

#1: *(Pause)* I don't think I like the way my character is developing.

#2: I knew it! OK, Let me start by reminding you that you're on a soap opera. Characters don't develop here, they just...are. That aside, how is your character's being, or lack thereof, affecting the whole show?!

#1: Hey, if I'm not happy with him/her, how can the show be any good?

#2: *(Pause)* You got me there, Sparky. I'm stumped. I guess I'll go to lunch and ponder your quandary.

#1: Is that good? What are you going to do about it?

#2: About what? Lunch? I don't know, I thought I'd start with a salad, then move on to the main course...

#1: No, I mean me. What about my needs? What about my wants?

#2: I know what you want, and as far as your needs go, I think you need to be quiet and stop complaining.

#1: I don't complain. I guess I just have to remind you that a star of my stature requires special handling.

#2: Great I'll put a sticker on you that says "This end up." *(Pause)* You are unbelievable. Is your memory that short, cause mine isn't. A year ago you were a walk-on-nobody with one line. By the time we were finished shooting you couldn't stop thanking me for my incredible direction and couldn't stop kissing my foot!

#1: Yeah, well now the kiss is on the other foot!

#2: *(Pause)* Do you practice saying stupid things like that?

#1: Fine, insult me, but in that year I've become the hottest star in daytime TV. I'm the man/woman you love to hate, quote, unquote. I've won an Emmy. What does that tell you?

#2: Nothing. They gave Marisa Tomei an Oscar. Same thing.

#1: OK, what about these? *(Takes a couple of tabloids out and puts them on the table.)* You think these magazines come after just anybody?

#2: I don't believe this, you are the only person I know who enjoys being in a tabloid.

#1: Do they write about you?

#2: No, and I'm broken hearted. Did you even read these? *(Picks up the magazines.)* This one says you had lunch with Elvis...on Pluto...

#1: How do you know I didn't?

#2: I'm going to ignore that. This one says you really are Newt Gingrich, and this one, *People,* printed your recipe for eggplant parmigiana. Yeah, you're quite the story.

#1: And you call me stupid. You don't get it. It's not the content, it's the fact that people want to know about me. Do you know how many magazines I've appeared in? One hundred and seventy-five.

#2: You actually counted?

#1: Of course and that's not including *TV Guide.* Maybe it's the *Enquirer* this week, next week it may be *Time.* Who knows. What's important is they ask. Can you say the same? *(#2 doesn't answer.)* I didn't think so. Maybe it's the reason you don't like me.

#2: No, that's not it. I don't like you because you're a pompous, self-involved, windbag of an actor/actress with bad hair, who likes to push other people around, has the acting talent of a sand flea and the IQ of a Frisbee.

#1: I beg your pardon, but I have perfect hair. And before you decide to get any more castic with me...

#2: Caustic.

#1: That's what I said, let me remind you of something. The

people don't tune in to watch the direction. They wouldn't know a close-up from a close out, they watch the show...and they love me. And so do the sponsors. I sell a heck of a lot of...whatever they make and right now — I'm very safe. And you can — take that to the bank!

#2: Know what, aside from saying castic, that's the smartest thing you've said in a year. But that too can change. See, my wife/husband is the head writer.

#1: In the last year I was arrested for the murder of my ex-husband/wife's sister's doctor and pulled out of the electric chair at the last moment. I was bitten by a black-headed Bushmaster in Central America and barely survived by doing a blood transfusion with a donkey. I was hit by lightning, died and came back, I got run over by a bus, survived, sued and became a millionaire. What more can you do to me?

#2: I can talk to my wife/husband and have him/her give you...a cough.

#1: *(Is dumbstruck.)* YOU WOULDN'T?!

#2: Wouldn't I?

#1: But you can't. It's not fair. You get a cough on this show and two weeks later it's pneumonia. Two weeks after that it's a rare tropical disease and two weeks after that...

#2: ...they're pulling the coffin out of the prop cabinet and you're registering with a temp agency.

#1: Please don't do this to me. *(Pause)* I'll do anything.

#2: Anything? Fine. 1: You learn your scripts — with your glasses on. 2: You show up on time. 3: I don't want to hear anymore about this "special handling" and 4: You generally stop being a pain. Agreed?

#1: Yes. Anything you say. Just don't give me a cough.

#2: Don't give me a reason to. Now go to lunch. You only have forty-five minutes left.

#1: I'll be back in forty. *(Runs off.)*

#2: Actors. They're such children.

25. The Speech

(In a hotel room. #1 and #2 are aides to a senator. They are helping to set up for a speech the next day. #1 and #2 are both on the phone.)

#1:

No, the Senator cannot be there at that time. *(Pause)* **He can make it after his speech tomorrow, but only for a few minutes.** *(Pause)* **Why? Because he's having dinner with the Governor later that night.** *(Pause)* **I'm glad we could clear that up.**

#2:

Yes the Senator does stand by that policy. *(Pause)* **No, he doesn't stand by that policy.** *(Pause)* **Why? He made that quite clear during his policy standing speech in Washington during free speech week, last week.** *(Pause)* **I'm glad we could clear that up.**

(#1 and #2 both hang up.)

#1: I hate these campaign trips.

#2: They're not that bad.

#1: Oh, you're so politically young. This is your first campaign. Trust me, by election time, you won't even want to vote for this guy.

#2: Well, I don't care. I've wanted to get into the game for a long time. Besides, why are you complaining? Everything seems to be going just...

#1: STOP! Don't even think that. Don't you know about the campaign jinx?

#2: What campaign jinx?

#1: You never say things are going well.

#2: Why not?

#1: Because the minute you do... *(The phone rings.)* See.

#2: How do you know it's bad news?

#1: Because you said things are going well. *(Picks up the phone.)* Yes. *(Pause)* No, I'm sorry, the Senator's very busy. *(Pause)* When did you talk to him? *(Pause)* Yes, I know, but that's not on the agenda. *(Pause)* Who authorized it? *(Pause)* But... *(Pause)* I know it's a very important organization, but... *(Pause)* but... *(Pause)* I see. Fine. *(Hangs up.)*

#2: Is there a problem?

#1: Yes, thanks to you.

#2: I didn't do anything. All I said was things were going well.

#1: That was enough.

#2: What's the problem?

#1: It appears that there's a OMWAM convention in town and they want the Senator to give a little speech.

#2: OMWAM?

#1: Organization of Mid-West American Mothers. They're a very important group that we need to have backing us.

#2: So what's the problem? When do they want the speech?

#1: In an hour. Apparently the Senator said he'd be glad to do it.

#2: So, let's talk to the Senator and have him postpone it a couple of hours.

#1: A couple of problems with that. First: OMWAM's luncheon is in an hour and secondly: the Senator's wife just got into town.

#2: So?

#1: He hasn't seen her in weeks.

#2: Again, so?

#1: They're saying hello...privately.

#2: *(Thinks and then finally gets it.)* Oh!

#1: Now, to top it off, OMWAM wants a crime speech.

They're big on that "keeping our streets safe for children" stuff.

#2: So, give him his crime speech.

#1: We don't have a current one and the speech for tomorrow is on health care.

#2: Where's his speech writer?

#1: On a plane. She's not due here for couple of hours.

#2: Can't he just wing it?

#1: Are you kidding?! Our boy's smart, but he couldn't ad-lib "you're welcome" after someone said, "thank you." We're gonna have to write one.

#2: I'm not a speech writer. I'm a press coordinator.

#1: Congratulations. You've just been promoted. *(Pause)* OK, look through all those papers and see if you can find our position paper on crime.

(#1 and #2 start looking through all the papers on the coffee table. #2 finds one.)

#2: I think this is it.

#1: Great! What's it say about the Senator's position on crime?

#2: He doesn't like it.

#1: "He doesn't like it?" Don't you think that'll come off as a bit anemic?

#2: Well, here's another one that says he really doesn't like it.

#1: Great. Well, I guess we'll have to go to the book.

#2: What book?

#1: *(Pulls a book out of his briefcase.)* This one. It's a book of great American speeches. We keep it around for emergencies like this.

#2: You use other people's speeches? That's terrible!

#1: Why? No one listens to them anyway. You remember that great speech the Senator gave at the convention?

#2: Yeah.

#1: John Kennedy's "Ask not what your country can do for

you..." **speech.** *(Starts flipping through the book, finally stopping.)* **Found it.** *(Hand the book to #2.)*

#2: *(Reads the speech.)* **This is the Gettysburg Address.**

#1: **Not by the time we're done with it. Get a pencil and sit down.** *(#2 grabs a pad and pencil and sits on the couch.)* *(Starts dictating the speech.)* **OK, let's see. "Four score and seven years ago, our fathers brought forth on this continent a new nation, conceived in liberty and dedicated to the proposition that all men are created equal." OK that becomes, "87 years ago our ancestors formed this great and powerful nation where everyone should be safe on our streets."**

#2: **Wow, that's good, but it was 87 years ago when Lincoln wrote this. Now it would be 218 years.**

#1: **Good point! See, you're a natural. Going on..."Now we are engaged in a great civil war..." yeah, yeah, yeah...let's say, "Now we're engaged in a great war on crime, testing whether our nation is strong enough to survive."**

#2: **You are good. Can I have a whack at it?**

#1: **Sure. We're right here.** *(Shows #2 the book.)* **The part about meeting on the battle field and dedicating it.**

#2: *(Thinks.)* **OK, how's this? "Today we meet here and in towns and cities all over this great country to dedicate the streets to those innocents who have fallen there."**

#1: **I am impressed! Keep going.**

#2: **"But we cannot dedicate these streets. Those who have lost their lives on American streets have dedicated them for themselves. Most of the world will not know or remember the thousands who have died, so it is up to us, the living, to make sure that this wave of violence ends. That is the task we are charged with. When it is finished those who have perished will not have died in vain. This is the only way we can make sure that this government of the people, by the people, and for the**

people, will not perish from the Earth!"

#1:   *(Stands and applauds.)* **What can I say? You're a master. Trust me, you're going a long way in politics. Type that up.** *(#2 goes to the typewriter and starts to type. The phone rings. #1 Gets the phone.)* **Yeah.** *(Pause)* **Uh-huh.** *(Pause)* **Uh-huh.** *(Pause)* **When.** *(Pause)* **Yeah, I should've figured.** *(Hangs up.)*

#2:   **What now?**

#1:   **OMWAM also wants our boy to talk about women's rights, too.**

(#1 and #2 think. Then look at each other.)

#1/#2: **The Declaration of Independence.**

(They both dive for the book.)

26. The Tabloid

(In an office. #1 is an editor for a not-too-reputable tabloid magazine. #1 is on the phone.)

#1: **Whoa, you wanna lower your voice.** *(Pause)* **Yes, I know you're a big star. Everyone knows you're a big star, but it's not my fault that you dated a chimpanzee.** *(Pulls the phone away from his/her ear.)* **You're yelling again.** *(Pause)* **It's not a lie. Do you remember that actress...uh...Marsha you dated in 1979?** *(Pause)* **Well, trust me, you did. Anyway, I checked and she was one of the chimps in the movie, "Murder on the Planet of the Chimpanzees."** *(Pause)* **So, she played a chimp, you dated her, you do the math.** *(Pause)* **If that's the way you feel, you know the number of our legal department.** *(Pause)* **Yeah, always nice to hear from you, Mr. Vontoken.** *(Hangs up then dials an extension.)* **Joe, expect a call from Vontoken.** *(Pause)* **Yeah, Mr. Vontoken said "He'd be back"** *(Pause)* **Anyway, handle it in the usual manner.** *(Hangs up.)*

#2: *(Knocks at the door.)* **You wanted to see me?**

#1: **Yeah, come on in. Have a seat.** *(#2 enters and sits in the chair in front of #1's desk.)* **So, how do you like working with us?**

#2: **Fine. I'm learning a lot. It's very different from what I expected.**

#1: **I know. They don't teach you this stuff in journalism school, huh?**

#2: **Uh...no, that's true.**

#1: **And just how long have you been with us?**

#2: **About six weeks.**

#1: **That long?**

#2: **Why? Is something wrong?**

#1: **No, no, I wouldn't say...wrong. Just...**

113

#2: Just what?

#1: It's just that I hoped you'd catch on a little faster.

#2: I'm sorry. I'm really trying and...

#1: Wait, don't panic. I like you. That's why we're having this talk. You just don't seem to totally get what we do here.

#2: What do you mean?

#1: *(Shuffles through some papers on his/her desk.)* Look, here's a good example. This is the story you handed in yesterday. It's about how you trailed Tom Burgess and his wife as they went to dinner and the movies. How they were in disguise, and so on and so on.

#2: So, what's wrong?

#1: Nothing's wrong. It's a nice little story. Thing is...we don't write nice little stories here. *(Hands #2 another story.)* Here's Dolan's story about Tom Burgess. Read the headline out loud.

#2: *(Takes the story and starts to read.)* "Tom Burgess seen in bed with little girl and goat!" WHAT?!

#1: Sort of catches your attention, doesn't it?

#2: But...how can you write this?

#1: You've worked with Dolan for a while. Tell me how she got this. Let me start you. She was home the other night...

#2: Think like Dolan. OK, how's this? Dolan was at home the other night...in bed, watching television. On one channel she sees a Burgess movie..."Break Through" and on another..."Little Women." So, doing the math you get Tom Burgess, a little girl and a goat being seen in bed."

#1: Pretty close. Actually, the other movie was, "Heidi."

#2: And actually, they were seen from bed, not in bed.

#1: In, from, we're talking about an adverb...

#2: Preposition.

#1: Whatever. The point is, by changing one little... preposition, we have something worth reading. Put this story on the cover, we'll sell a million papers.

#2: But it's misleading and we'll get sued.

#1: And your point is?

#2: We'll — get — sued!

#1: In the six weeks you've been here do you know how many times we've been sued?

#2: No.

#1: 183. We get sued like other companies order in lunch. It's what we do.

#2: But it's not journalism.

#1: It's not supposed to be. You want journalism, work for a newspaper.

#2: So we don't actually report the news here. We manufacture it?

#1: Exactly! And it's really much more fun. We create entertainment.

#2: Is that ethical?

#1: Who cares, it's profitable. *(Grabs a photo and gives it to #2.)* What do you see in that picture?

#2: Madonna making out with some guy at Spago.

#1: Right, but everyone's got a picture of Madonna making out with someone. What's interesting is the table next to hers. What do you see?

#2: Two guys having lunch.

#1: OK, now look closely at the guy on the right. Who does he look like?

#2: *(Looks closely at the photo.)* I don't know...I guess, President Kennedy a little.

#1: That's what we thought. Now the guy on the left, the one with the long hair. How about him?

#2: With that look, he could be a rock musician.

#1: Could be, but look again. Shoulder length hair, sort of a flowing type shirt...think biblical. What do you get?

#2: *(Thinks and then gets a realization.)* Oh, no. You're not thinking...Moses?

#1: *(Smiles and shrugs.)* How do we know it's not?

#2: So you're saying this is a picture of Moses and John

Kennedy having lunch at Spago?

#1: Could be.

#2: And if we blow up that section of the photo, blur it a bit, superimpose some tablets on the table we...

#1: We've got a story.

#2: That's ridiculous!

#1: No more than the story we ran on the three-headed baby...or... Dan Quayle talking to Martians. *(Pause)* OK, maybe not Dan Quayle.

#2: But...

#1: No buts. Assume that these two did have lunch. What would they talk about?

#2: How easy it was for them to get a reservation.

#1: Possibly, but what else?

#2: I don't know, world peace...the state of the country...the necessity of carrying an umbrella.

#1: The point is, it's up to you. I want 600 words from you, by closing, about this lunch meeting.

#2: *(Starts to exit. He/she comes back to the desk.)* I'm not sure if you noticed, but Kennedy is picking up the check. Is that because he always had more money than Moses?

#1: You tell me.

#2: And what am I supposed to call this story? Last Lunch?

#1: "Last Lunch." I like that. It'll make a great slammer. You write this right and you'll have the headline. Now go and create some news. *(#2 exits. #1 gets on the phone.)* Yeah, change the headline to "Last Lunch." You'll have the story in a couple of hours. Also, call legal and tell them Tom Burgess will probably be calling in a couple of days. *(Pause)* Hey, it's not our fault that the guy likes goats...

27. The Teacher

(A teacher's lounge. #1 is pouring a cup of coffee. He/she then sits down, picks up a paper and starts to read. #2 comes running in and slams the door.)

#2: **Please hide me! Don't let them get me!** *(Dives behind the couch.)*

#1: *(Puts down his/her paper.)* **That was a heck of an entrance. I can't wait to see how you exit.**

#2: *(Pops up from behind the couch.)* **I'm happy you find this amusing. You wouldn't be so glib if it were you they were after.**

#1: **Who is they?**

#2: **Who do you think! Those...horrors. Those...creatures, those...vermin, those...**

#1: **Children?**

#2: **You have the audacity to call them that?**

#1: **That's what they are. They're high school students. Nothing more.**

#2: **That's like saying a Great White shark is a fish and nothing more.**

#1: **Well, from some people's point of view, that's correct.**

#2: **Then you must have gotten the only "students" in the school. The rest of us seem to have gotten what was left over.**

#1: **You wanna tell me what brought all this on...today.**

#2: **The usual. Why do you think anything would be different?**

#1: **Because you usually don't run shrieking from your classroom.**

#2: **Not usually, but I think about it a lot.** *(Pause)* **OK, aside from the usual noise, back talk, loud music, smoking in the bathroom, et cetera, at one point today I found a sign taped to my back.**

117

#1:   So, they've been doing that since Socrates was teaching. **What did it say? "Kick me"?** *(#2 takes a piece of paper out of a pocket and hands it to #1. #1 unfolds it and reads it.)* **"Kill me, suck the marrow from my bones and incinerate the rest."** *(Pause)* **Well, it's descriptive.**

#2:   **Enough said?**

#1:   **OK, but you've completely overlooked the bright side.**

#2:   **There's a bright side to this?**

#1:   **Yes. Whoever wrote this actually knows what bone marrow is and...even spelled incinerate right. See?**

#2:   **My but you're just a regular "glass is half full" kind of guy/gal, aren't you?**

#1:   **I'm just realistic. You're mistaking that for optimism.**

#2:   **Look all I know is that when I was in college, studying to be a teacher, I was told that when I came into the classroom, the students would sit, listen, and learn.**

#1:   **Where did you go to college? Laura Ingalls University? This is what I'm talking about. That's not a realistic expectation.**

#2:   **Then what is?**

#1:   **You go in, impart whatever knowledge you have and let whoever wants to suck it up, do so.**

#2:   *(Just stares at #1. Pause)* **That's the most asinine thing I've ever heard. Don't you find that a slightly cavalier approach to teaching?**

#1:   **Maybe, but most of my students seem to enjoy my class.**

#2:   **You teach gym! Only the spastics don't like gym. You have no knowledge to impart, so you're home free. I'm a math teacher.**

#1:   **Yeah, well, that does kind of start you off in the debit column.**

#2:   **And you know what, that's not even the bad part. I know most kids hate math, but there are some who don't and it's great when they learn. My real problem seems to be that I've lost control of my classes. My kids are pretty unruly.**

#1:   Oh, that. That's a whole different story. That's a matter of attitude.

#2:   I know. Their attitudes could use a lot work.

#1:   Not their attitude, yours. Let's try a test. Stand over there and pretend you're teaching. I'll be one of your students who's standing in the back of the room, talking.

#2:   *(Walks a few feet away.)* So, if you bisect the triangle at the base at a 90 degree angle, you get...

#1:   *(Stands and turns like he/she is talking to someone.)* Anyway, Suzy and I are going to the mall tonight...

#2:   *(Goes over to #1.)* Excuse me, I'm trying to teach a class here.

#1:   So?

#2:   So, I'd appreciate it if you'd stop talking and sit down.

#1:   Yeah? Well, I'd appreciate if you'd shut up!

#2:   I...I...you...

#1:   See, I've got you stuttering already. Here, let's switch places and let me show you how to do it. *(The two switch places and start the experiment over.)* So, the sit-up first began in ancient Greece with Sitius Upus...

#2:   Bob and I are going to the movies tonight...

#1:   *(Walks over to #2.)* Excuse me, I'm trying to teach here.

#2:   So?

#1:   So, if you don't shut up and sit down in that chair, I'm going make you sorry your mother and father ever met each other. *(#2 drops into a chair, mouth agape, staring at #1.)* See. Now you're in your chair and quiet.

#2:   Oh, please tell me that you don't really say that to your students.

#1:   Why shouldn't I?

#2:   Aside from the fact it's just a touch on the rude side?

#1:   Well relax. I don't, but with my attitude, I may as well. See, it's in the eyes, the voice, the tone. Get it? Authority is all up here. *(Points to his/her head.)*

#2:   So I have to make them think I'm tough.

119

#1: Exactly. These kids are terrified of me. They think I'm a psycho.

#2: And you think that's a good way for them to feel?

#1: I think it's the only way they should feel.

#2: How do they feel about me?

#1: They call you "welcome" behind your back.

#2: What's that mean?

#1: You know...welcome – as in door mat.

#2: Oh. That's not good. What should I do?

#1: Toughen up mentally. Make them think you'll rip their spleens out if they don't listen. Say it with your eyes, your voice.

#2: OK, how's this? *(Screws up his/her face trying to look tough and barks at #1.)* OK...you...you sit your buttocks in that chair or...or...you'll regret it! Deeply! And...I'm not kidding.

(A pause.)

#1: Yeah, OK, well... it's a start. Are you free this period?

#2: Yes.

#1: You should go back to your room and practice. It makes perfect you know.

#2: I think I will. Thanks for all your help.

#1: No problem. That's what I'm here for.

#2: *(Starts to exit practicing.)* You sit down...sit down now, I'll...make you sorry if you don't... *(Turns to #1 and tries to be mean.)* I'm tough so don't fudge with me!

#1: Great. Just...great. Keep practicing. *(#2 exits while continuing to practice. #1 watches until he/she is gone.)* He'll/She'll be dead in two minutes. *(Pause)* Oh well, c'est la vie. *(Picks the paper back up and continues to read.)*

Section Two:
DRAMA

28. Acceptance

(We are in an apartment. #1 is sitting on the couch reading. There is a knock on the door. #1 answers it. #2 is standing there.)

#1: You look awful.

#2: Can I come in?

#1: Yeah. Come on in.

#2: *(Enters and goes to the couch and sits.)* I'm sorry if I'm taking you from anything.

#1: I was just reading. What is it? What's wrong?

#2: *(Pause)* She's/He's gone.

#1: Who's gone?

#2: Who do you think? Jenny/Jerry!

#1: What do you mean, he's/she's gone?

#2: How many definitions of "gone" do you know? I couldn't get him/her at work all day and he/she wasn't at home either.

#1: So, maybe Jenny/Jerry took the day off. Went to a movie, took...

#2: *(Cuts #1 off.)* I thought that, too. When I got home, the house was empty.

#1: Maybe he's/she's still out.

#2: No, I don't mean no one's there. I mean it was emptied out. Everything was gone.

#1: Everything?

#2: Except the bed, my living room chair, the refrigerator...a few other things.

#1: Oh.

#2: I also called the bank and half our account was cleaned out. And if that weren't enough, I'm taking all this in and a guy comes to the door and serves me with divorce papers. They were filed two weeks ago but requested not to be served until today.

#1: I see.

#2: What am I going to do?

#1: Let me ask you this, what does Jenny/Jerry want from you?

#2: Nothing. He/She just wants me to sign the papers. You know, no fault divorce. He's/She's found somebody else.

#1: How do you know?

#2: *(Pulls out a letter and hands it to #1.)* I finally found this in the bedroom. *(#1 reads the letter. When done, #1 hands the letter back to #2.)* What do you think?

#1: I think that if you don't want anything back that he/she took, you should sign the papers.

#2: What?

#1: I think it's what's best. For both of you.

#2: *(Pause)* Wait a minute. You don't seem surprised. You knew about this, didn't you?

#1: Everyone knew about this.

#2: What are you talking about?

#1: All you had to do was look at you two and you knew it was going bad.

#2: Is this your definition of support?

#1: Hey, I'll give you all the support you want, but it won't change what I feel. You guys had a marriage in name only.

#2: And you're so sure of that?

#1: I probably shouldn't have said that. It really doesn't matter what I think.

#2: Sorry, you can't just drop a line like that and let it go. What do you mean that I had a marriage in name only?

#1: You really want to do this now?

#2: Yes!

#1: Why?

#2: Because I don't understand what's going on and if you think you have any ideas I'd really like to know.

#1: Fine. Let me ask you this. When's the last time you and

Jenny/Jerry actually had any fun?

#2: We went out a lot.

#1: That's not what I mean. When's the last time you two had fun alone. Just the two of you. Not at a party, but at home, having dinner, watching TV, renting a video, going to the movies. Just enjoyed being with each other?

#2: OK, I know what you mean, but we...we both were working ...a lot, we...

#1: I rest my case.

#2: Hold on! Just because we didn't cuddle on the couch every night, doesn't mean that we had a bad marriage.

#1: No, but the fact that you can't remember the last time you did is quite a symptom. But let's put that aside, your husband/wife left you. Shouldn't that drive the point home pretty loud and clear? Just because you didn't see it doesn't make it any less valid.

#2: And you don't see this as the coward's way out? Sneaking out when I wasn't around.

#1: How would you have it? Is a screaming battle in the middle of your apartment better? This is what he/she wanted. Re-read this letter. He/she wants to talk, but you both need time first.

#2: I don't need any time because I don't think it's over. I think we can be saved.

#1: But it takes more than you to make it a couple. Jerry/Jenny has to be in agreement. What are you really trying to save here? Your pride?

#2: No, it's not that.

#1: Then what?

#2: I need her/him in my life. We've been together since we were kids. We grew up together. If I think of any facet of my life, she's/he's there. I just can't dismiss that. Pretend that it never happened.

#1: No one's asking you to. Maybe everyone expected you two to get married when you should have just been friends. I

125

don't know. It seems to me that you grew up together and now you've grown apart. It's no one's fault. It happens.

#2: I just can't walk away from that.

#1: You don't have to, but you can't force something that isn't there.

#2: So what am I supposed to do?

#1: Sign the papers. If you really want to keep him/her in your life, you have to cut free the part that's dead and let what's left grow.

#2: *(Trying to hold it together.)* It's...hard. It's very hard.

#1: I know, but I think in the long run, it's really for the best.

#2: It's gonna take some time to convince me of that.

#1: I know. *(Pause)* Hey, why don't we go out and get you some groceries and stuff for your apartment.

#2: I'm not really hungry.

#1: You will be sometime. Besides, the walk will do you good.

#2: Why will a walk do me good?

#1: *(Pause)* I don't know. That's what they always do in the movies.

(They both chuckle a bit.)

#2: Well, far be it from me to contradict Hollywood. Let's go for a walk.

(#1 grabs a jacket and they head for the door and exit.)

29. Privacy

(In a restaurant. #1, a reporter, is sitting at a table. #2 enters, looks around, sees #1, goes over to the table, and throws a newspaper in front of him/her.)

#1: Usually I have this delivered to my house, but thanks.

#2: You want to explain this?

#1: *(Picks up the paper and looks at it.)* Well, it's a newspaper and they're black and white and read all over. I work for one. *(Pause)* This one, as a matter of fact. Does that clear it up? *(Holds the paper out to #2.)*

#2: I want to know where you got this story!

#1: Sorry, my sources are confidential.

#2: That's great. Some liar gets confidentiality and my life is all over this rag?

#1: Hey, you chose a profession that puts you in the public eye. You know that, so don't blame me if you can't handle the consequences.

#2: Oh, I can handle the public eye. What's abhorrent is printing bald-faced lies. That's obviously your job.

#1: Everything I wrote is the truth as far as I know.

#2: Yeah, well you don't know anything and that's the truth!

#1: Fine, then enlighten me.

#2: Go to hell! *(Starts to exit.)*

#1: This is why I had to rely on other sources for this story instead of you.

#2: What are you talking about?

#1: When I first heard about this, I tried to get in touch with you to talk about it.

#2: I never got a call from you.

#1: Well then talk to your publicist. I called her and she said that you had no comment and were too busy to talk. So, I was left to my own devices.

#2: When was this?

#1: A week or two ago.

#2: First off, I had no comment because I never heard any rumors about this, and secondly, I was too busy. I was filming a movie and I told my publicist I didn't want to do any interviews until we wrapped. I had a job to do. Is that so difficult to understand?

#1: Not at all, but understand that I also have a job to do. I cover the entertainment scene. So, I guess we both did what we had to.

#2: Except that my job is make believe. I don't try and pass off innuendo, hearsay, and appearance as the truth. I also wouldn't hurt an innocent bystander.

#1: Hey, I'm not the one running around on my spouse in public.

#2: Neither am I!

#1: Well, that's what I was told by my sources!

#2: Oh yeah, your "confidential sources." Just for your information, that poor little production assistant you paid to give you information from the set made a mistake and shot off his mouth. From what he told us before he was fired was that you said you were just looking for some harmless little gossip items. Nobody would be hurt. What was that, just a little harmless white lie?

#1: Yeah, well...

#2: Well, nothing! That kid will probably never work again. So there's another notch for your gun.

#1: You know what's amazing? When you all are starting out as struggling actors you beg for publicity. You have no idea what I've been offered by actors, agents, managers, publicists, to get your names in the paper. Then when the few of you do make it big, you turn around and spit on me for giving you exactly the same thing. I'd call you all schizophrenic, but I think hypocritical says it better.

#2: OK, you've got a point. But when does it stop? What part of my life is off limits?

#1: I'd have to say...none.

#2: I suppose asking for a retraction is out of the question?

#1: Tell me why.

#2: What's going on is nobody's business but mine.

#1: Sorry, that's not good enough.

#2: *(Thinks for a moment.)* OK, look, I'll tell you my reasons, but this conversation is off the record. If my reasons are valid to you, then print a retraction, without details. Just say you were wrong. If not, at least don't follow up on the story. I'm asking this as a favor.

#1: You've never given me problems before – OK, deal.

#2: I suppose you want to know who the man/woman I've been seen with is.

#1: That would be a good place to start.

#2: Well, he/she is my brother/sister. *(#1 looks at #2.)* What? You don't believe me?

#1: It's not that, it's just that in my business, that's the same as introducing someone as your "niece"/"nephew."

#2: OK, I see where you're at, but that person is my brother/sister.

#1: Then why didn't you introduce him/her to anyone? Why were you sneaking her/him into your dressing room and locking the door?

#2: Your "source" was good. I wasn't sneaking anyone. I just wanted some privacy.

#1: Why?

#2: He's/she's a doctor.

#1: Are you sick?

#2: No.

#1: Then who?

#2: *(Pause)* My wife/husband.

#1: I'm...I'm sorry.

#2: My brother/sister is counseling us on the best course of treatment, which doctors to see. That sort of thing. My wife/husband doesn't want me to stop working because there's nothing I can really do.

#1: I understand.

#2: Unfortunately, that means I can't always go with her/him to his/her appointments. When that happens my brother/sister would come to the studio or we'd meet for lunch and she/he would fill me in.

#1: If I can ask...how is she/he doing?

#2: OK. She/he has his/her rough days, but we're determined to beat this.

#1: There's a lot of people out there who would give you support.

#2: I know and I appreciate it, but...

#1: But what.

#2: I've always tried to keep my family out of my spotlight. This is not about me and we'd like to deal with it on our own. Is that really too much to ask?

#1: No, it's not. You know, you could have saved us both a lot of trouble by telling me this before.

#2: Maybe, but as you mentioned, I'm a public figure. How many details of my private life can I trust anyone with?

#1: *(Pause)* I get your point. *(Pause)* I'll print the retraction.

#2: My wife/husband will appreciate it. *(Starts to leave.)*

#1: I am sorry.

#2: *(Stops and looks at #1.)* You know, I think you are. Who would have thought? *(Exits.)*

30. The Accident

(A holding room of a county jail. #1 is sitting at a table waiting. #2 enters and sits.)

#1: How are you feeling?

#2: How do I look?

#1: Pretty awful.

#2: That's how I'm feeling. How long till I can get out of here?

#1: We have to talk.

#2: Fine. Post the bail, get me out of here and we'll go have coffee and talk.

#1: I'm afraid it's not that easy.

#2: What? What's the problem? I've had DUIs before.

#1: That's just the point. You're a repeat offender. They're not looking on you very favorably.

#2: Who cares how they see me. My parents have friends and money. That's all that counts.

#1: Not this time. Not with an accident involved.

#2: *(Pause)* There was, wasn't there?

#1: How drunk were you?

#2: I guess very. How's my car?

#1: How's your car?! Is that all you have to say?

#2: I'm sorry. I didn't mean it to sound like that. I just don't remember.

#1: Then let me refresh your memory. You got drunk, got behind the wheel, slammed into a car with a mother and daughter going home, and drove their car into a brick wall.

#2: I didn't know. I'm sorry. I'm sure my parents will pay for any medical costs.

#1: Money can't buy you out of this one.

#2: Look, it may cost a little more, but I'm sure we can get out of it.

#1:   *(Pause)* You really don't know. What do you think you're being charged with?

#2:   A DUI, I guess endangerment, having an accident. I don't know. You're the first person I've talked to since I called last night.

#1:   Then let me spell it out to you. The little girl in the car, she died this morning. The mother is in critical condition and they don't know if she's going to make it. So aside from the other charges, you're being charged with at least one count of vehicular manslaughter. Possibly two.

#2:   Oh, no.

#1:   Now maybe you're seeing the whole picture. So the best thing you can do right now is shut up, drop the superiority act and realize that there's no quick out on this one.

#2:   So...what am I looking at?

#1:   I think it's pretty safe to say that you are going to do some jail time.

#2:   *(Starts to panic.)* No! No, you cannot let that happen.

#1:   You still don't get it. It has nothing to do with me. The courts are going to throw the book at you. While you were in here sleeping it off last night, they were splashing pictures of the accident all over the 11:00 news.

#2:   What does that mean?

#1:   People are upset. No one wants to see you walk on this. Especially when they find out who your family is.

#2:   Can't my parents do anything?

#1:   You want the truth?

#2:   Yes.

#1:   Your parents aren't going to do a thing this time.

#2:   What?

#1:   They're not going to bail you out.

#2:   Why not?

#1: Why not? I can't believe you just asked that question.

#2: So they're just going to let me go to jail.

#1: In your father's words: "It's just what he/she deserves."

#2: I don't believe it.

#1: Hey, maybe it's time you grasped reality. You killed a person. Maybe two. Nobody can just dismiss that. Not even your parents.

#2: And you're just going to sit there and let this happen?

#1: OK, listen to me. When your father called I told him I didn't want anything to do with this one. I said I thought you should go straight to jail. It wasn't until he agreed with me that I said I'd come down here.

#2: So, why are you here?

#1: It's a favor. They want you to be punished, but they don't want you hurt. I said I'd try and make a deal with the DA to get you sent somewhere, where at least you'll be safe.

#2: What if I don't agree?

#1: You have no choice! Go ahead, fire me, take your chances with a public defender. But God only knows where you'll wind up. 'Cause believe me when I tell you, you are going away.

#2: OK, you listen to me. I cannot go to jail. I won't survive. I can't be locked up with...people like that.

#1: What the hell are you? You are people like that. You killed someone. That hardly makes you citizen of the year.

#2: It's not the same thing. I had an accident.

#1: No, you were an accident. Just waiting to happen. I'm just surprised it took this long.

#2: I can't have my life taken away like this!

#1: What about the life of that little girl? Huh?! She was five years old. People will walk by her grave and comment on how young she was and what a shame it is. What about her mother and father? You took their little girl!

#2: You're talking like I did it on purpose.

#1: You did, in a sense.

133

#2:   How can you say that?

#1:   How many times have you been arrested for drunk driving? How many programs have you gone through? None of it mattered. You just didn't care!

#2:   You're happy about this. Aren't you?

#1:   Someone's dead. How can I be happy? What I feel is guilty.

#2:   What are you guilty about?

#1:   Because I got you off those other times. Maybe if you had done some jail time, or had been locked up in some clinic, that little girl would still alive.

#2:   I see now. You don't like me and you want to see me put away.

#1:   You're right, I don't like you. I think you're a waste and you're getting what you deserve.

#2:   Why, because I have money?

#1:   Stop trying to see yourself as some put-upon minority. A lot of people have money. You cavalierly go about doing whatever you please without thought one to anyone else and now it's come crashing in on you.

#2:   What am I going to do?

#1:   Try accepting some responsibility for once. Try apologizing to your parents and the family of that little girl. I don't know. You figure it out. *(Rises and starts to exit.)*

#2:   Where are you going?

#1:   You're being arraigned in two hours. I'm going to talk to the DA and see what I can do.

#2:   Please help me. I'm terrified.

#1:   Good! *(Exits.)*

31. The Agreement

(In a restaurant. #1 is sitting at a table having a drink.
#1 checks the time. #2 enters and goes over to #1's table.)

#1: You're late!

#2: I wouldn't have come at all, except your voice-mail message sounded very ominous.

#1: It wasn't ominous.

#2: No? Then what would you call a message that says; "I'll be at Mario's at 12:30. It would be in your best interest to meet me there."

#1: I'd call it watching out for a friend.

#2: Maybe, if we were friends. What do you want?

#1: Oh, relax. Sit down and have a drink.

#2: *(Sits.)* I don't want a drink, I don't want to relax, but I do want to get out of here. What do you want?

#1: OK – we can play this any way you want.

#2: Just get on with it. I've got a lot of work to do.

#1: I'm sure you know that Matt Johnson is retiring.

#2: So?

#1: Well, his Vice-President spot is opening up and I want it.

#2: Yeah, you've got a prayer.

#1: Actually, I have much more than that.

#2: How's that?

#1: Because you're going to help me get it.

#2: Sure I am. Right after I get back from my vacation on the moon.

#1: Then blast off. I'm serious.

#2: You know what's so funny? I don't like you, which everyone knows, and I don't think you're qualified for the job you have now. So why would I lift a finger to get you promoted?

#1: *(Reaches into the briefcase, pulls out a large envelope and hands it to #2.)* Because of this.

#2:   **What is it?**

#1:   **Open it.**

#2:   *(Opens the envelope, looks at the documents and is somewhat taken aback.)* **How did you get these?**

#1:   **That's not important. I have them.**

#2:   **What are you planning?**

#1:   **That all depends on you.**

#2:   **Meaning?**

#1:   **At next week's board meeting you are going to bring up my name as a replacement for Johnson and give me your personally written recommendation. Don't worry, it won't have to be too glowing. We wouldn't want to overdo it.**

#2:   **And if I don't?**

#1:   **Then Mr. Cromwell is going to get this packet and an anonymous letter detailing how his up-and-coming vice-president is selling company secrets to our competitors. I don't know our CEO too well, but I have a hunch he won't take this news lying down.**

#2:   **You can kiss my...**

#1:   **Fine! And you can kiss your career good-bye.**

#2:   **You're bluffing.**

#1:   **The unemployment office opens at eight A.M.** *(Gets up and starts to leave.)*

#2:   *(Leans across the table and pulls #1 back down.)* **Just who do you think you are?! I have worked my fingers to the bone and I'm not going to let my life go down the tubes because some unqualified fly-by-night can't cut it in the business world.**

#1:   **I can't cut it?! I'm not the one photocopying files and selling them to the highest bidder. Is that in some class I missed at Wharton's?**

#2:   **You have no idea what this is all about.**

#1:   **Oh I think I do. Let's see, you came here with an MBA from Harvard. Started working and got mad that you weren't advancing fast enough and being passed over. So** you decided to take matters into your own hands. Then when you finally did make Vice President, the "extra" money was too good to let go.

#2: You're wrong!

#1: Look, I'm a lot of things, but stupid isn't one of them. When I first came here I knew it would be rough, but after awhile I started to get along with everyone. Except you. Then I started hearing all the things you said behind my back to the suits...

#2: That's just office gossip...

#1: No it's not! So I checked you out and when I saw that the "golden one" was a little tarnished I saw my chance to protect myself.

#2: "Protect yourself"? You're just the same as I am. Fine, I'll admit that I took an...opportunity, but as far as you were concerned — you weren't qualified and, bottom line, you were getting in my way!

#1: Well now you're in mine.

#2: Cut to the chase.

#1: I already told you. I want Johnson's job and you off my back. There is no negotiation because I've got you by the...well, I've got you. You know it and I know it!

#2: And when you get the promotion?

#1: You get your files back. Deal?

#2: *(Stands.)* No, it's not a deal, but...I'll do it.

#1: I know.

#2: *(Starts to leave.)* I'll write the recommendation this afternoon. OK, Donato?

#1: Miss/Ms./Mr. Donato.

#2: What?

#1: It's Miss/Ms./Mr. Donato and don't forget it.
(#1 watches #2 exit. #1 smiles and takes a drink.)

32. The Campaign

(In a Senator's office. At the desk is the senator's campaign coordinator. At present he/she is going over some files and not happy about what he/she sees. #1 pushes the intercom.)

#1: Mathews, get in here.
(Mathews enters. He/she is an aide.)

#2: You rang?

#1: What is this? *(Throws the file on the floor.)*

#2: *(Looks at it.)* The latest election poll figures.

#1: So you're not a total idiot. Now, why don't you pick them up and read them to me.

#2: Why?

#1: Because I said so.

#2: *(Opens the folder and reads.)* "Senator Campbell – sixty-five percent, Congresswoman Meyers – thirty percent, City Councilman Frye – five percent."

#1: Good, you can read. Now, what's wrong with those figures?

#2: Nothing as far as I can see.

#1: Look again and compare them to last week's numbers.

#2: *(Checks both pages.)* Oh, I see. Our numbers have remained the same, Meyers gained a point and Frye's lost a point.

#1: Now answer me this, if Frye lost one point, why did Meyers get it and not us?

#2: You're joking, right?

#1: Do you hear me laughing?

#2: It's one point. We have sixty-five percent of the vote, we're leading by thirty-five percent, what difference could one point swapped between second and third place possibly mean?

#1: Maybe it means that someone is not doing his/her job.

#2: Hey, my team has the Senator on the verge of his widest re-election margin ever. So don't even insinuate that I'm not doing my job!

#1: I'm not insinuating anything, I'm stating a fact. If your team was doing all it could, that one point would have gone from Frye to us.

#2: It's one point!

#1: And what if she keeps gaining points?

#2: There's five weeks until the election. If she gained a point a week and we lost a point a week, it would still be a landslide.

#1: So that's how you see it?

#2: That's exactly how I see it! Congresswoman Meyers is going to lose, and she's going to lose big.

#1: I don't want her to "lose big," I want her to be humiliated! *(Silence.)*

#2: Why?

#1: Listen to the wind. Senator Campbell, in the not-too-distant future, is probably going to be president. I want it known that anyone who stands in his way will be crushed. Not beaten, crushed! It all comes down to power.

#2: Whose power? His or yours?

#1: What are you implying?

#2: Come on, if the senator becomes president, you'll most likely be a high ranking administrative official. That's where your power is.

#1: Maybe, but that's my concern. Yours is Meyers.

#2: Fine. I'll take care of it. *(Starts to leave.)*

#1: Where are you going?

#2: I thought you wanted me to take care of Meyers.

#1: I do and here's how we're going to do it. *(Pulls out a folder.)* I've been given some information that Meyers had a baby ten years ago and it died shortly after birth.

#2: It's not a secret.

#1: But what everyone doesn't know is that Meyers was

suspected of neglect by the police.

#2: **Where did you get that information?!**

#1: **Where do you think?**

#2: **Since I've never heard that before, I'm forced to believe that you made it up.**

#1: **Very good.**

#2: **What are you planning?**

#1: **Somehow this information is going to "leak" out. Then we'll sit back and see what happens.**

#2: **You're insane.**

#1: **Not at all. Most people won't believe it, but it will cause some doubt. And that doubt will translate into falling numbers.**

#2: **What do you think? That there's not going to be a denial?**

#1: **Of course there will be, but it doesn't matter.**

#2: **The woman lost a child. Something she'll never get over and you want to destroy the rest of her life. Just like that? Where's your conscience?**

#1: **Who are you, Jiminy Cricket? I do, what is necessary to get the job done. Get used to it. That's the way things work.**

#2: **And the Senator's OK with this?**

#1: **The senator doesn't know.**

#2: **He'll blow a gasket.**

#1: **Of course, and that's the beauty of all this.**

#2: **What?**

#1: **The senator will be furious. He'll launch an investigation, I'll tell him an over-zealous worker released it, we'll fire the jerk, the Senator will apologize and everything will be fine. Except that the damage will be done. It's perfect.**

#2: **And who's the patsy you plan to fire.**

#1: *(Stares at #2.)* **Don't worry, you'll be well compensated.**

#2: **WHAT?!**

#1: **As long as you keep your mouth shut.**

#2: **Let me get this straight, you're going to ruin Congresswoman Meyers and me for the sake of a few percentage** points that don't mean anything?

#1: In a New York minute. I don't care about Meyers...or you. You're both pretty insignificant.

#2: I don't think so.

#1: We're not paying you to think.

#2: As of this moment, you're not paying me at all. *(Starts to leave.)*

#1: Where do you think you're going?

#2: To let the Senator know what kind of lunatic is on his staff.

#1: Don't try it. First, he won't believe you and secondly...I'll destroy you.

#2: You can try.

#1: No, I can do it...and you know it. Now, get out. You're fired!

#2: Fine, you fired me, I quit, I really don't care. I'm out of here. But let me tell you one thing. If I go down, you're going with me.

#1: What movie did you pull that tired cliché from?

#2: Go ahead, be as glib as you want, but you haven't heard the last from me.

#1: Oh, I'm sure I have. Excuse me. *(Pushes an intercom button.)* Security, I'm having a problem. Could I get some assistance? Please? *(To #2)* Have a nice day.

33. The Case

(In an office. #1 is working at his/her desk. He/she is very engrossed in what they are doing. #1 pokes his/her head in the door and knocks. #1 looks up.)

#2: Hey. How you doing?

#1: OK.

#2: Busy?

#1: Depends on your definition of busy. Let's just say that I have enough work to keep me occupied for...oh, I don't know, the rest of my life.

#2: Can I come in for a minute?

#1: Sure. *(#2 comes in and sits down. There is a pause.)*

#2: Is that the Jenner case?

#1: Have I worked on anything else in the last four months?

#2: No, you haven't. I want to tell you that everyone thinks you've done a great job with this case. We wouldn't be as far as we are without you.

#1: *(Leans back in his/her chair.)* Why do I get the feeling that there's a "but" attached to the end of that statement?

#2: Because there is.

#1: Are you going to tell me or should I guess? Here, let me make it easier for you. "You've done a great job on this case, but..."

#2: You've done a great job, but I want you to put it aside. I've got another project for you. *(Starts to get up and leave.)*

#1: Wait a minute, wait a minute. What do you mean, "put it aside"? I thought you liked my work.

#2: I do. *(Pause)* We're dropping the case.

#1: You're what?!

#2: We're dropping the case.

#1: Just like that?

#2: Not just like that. We've been talking about it for a week.

#1:   So, why am I just now hearing about it and why don't I have any input?

#2:   Because when the District Attorney makes a decision, assistant DAs don't have a lot to say about it. Including me.

#1:   Then just give me the *Reader's Digest* version. Why?

#2:   We can't win.

#1:   Not true! Tell me honestly. Did I screw this up somehow?

#2:   No, I told you, we have all the confidence in the world in you. What we don't have anymore is a witness.

#1:   What are you talking about? I just talked with Kathy Jenner and her parents last week about her testimony.

#2:   I know and this morning her father called and told me that he's decided that Kathy shouldn't testify. He wants her to put this whole little mess behind her.

#1:   Little mess?! The girl was abused. He calls that "a little mess"?

#2:   Let's just say he was convinced to change his mind.

#1:   *(Pause)* How much were they paid?

#2:   Enough. End of story.

#1:   No, not "end of story." We cannot just let this guy get away with abusing a 14 year old. And I don't care how big a celebrity he is.

#2:   Well, because he is so big, he can afford to show the Jenners that time and money can heal all wounds.

#1:   That stinks!

#2:   I couldn't agree more. *(Starts to leave.)*

#1:   So you and the District Attorney are content to just let it end this way?

#2:   *(Stops and turns back.)* No, we are not! But our hands are tied. No witness, no case. Period!

#1:   It's not as simple as that.

#2:   Yes, it is. Look, we are not going to spend millions of taxpayer dollars to lose. The District Attorney will look bad, I'll look bad, you'll look bad...it's a no win situation.

#1:   So what are you saying? That we did all this work so we could have the appearance of propriety?

#2:   Would you please cut out all this sanctimonious crap and listen to me? We went after this guy and we went after him hard. We can't fight the fact that Harold Jenner is a scumbag who puts a dollar, or several million, over the well-being of his daughter.

#1:   Well, I can't let it end like this.

#2:   What are you going to do? You did the best you could. You made a big impression on the public...and this office. Just cut your losses and let it go.

#1:   Do you think I did this for publicity? To make myself look good? Coming to the DA's office was not a lucrative career move. I have no political ambitions. I just wanted to make a difference.

#2:   Didn't we all?

#1:   What the hell does that mean?

#2:   Sorry. It's not as jaded as it sounds.

#1:   I hope not.

#2:   Look, when I came here, I felt the same way you do.

#1:   So what happened?

#2:   Reality. I have a sign hanging on my wall that was a present from my old law professor. It's a quote from a book that says, "The study of the law is divine, the practice of the law is obscene."

#1:   And that's supposed to make me feel better?

#2:   I didn't say that. It's a suggestion that you look at things the way they really are.

#1:   I know how things are. Simply put, there are a lot of bad people out there, doing a lot of bad things.

#2:   That's right and no matter how hard you try, you can't stop them all or even punish all the ones you catch.

#1:   And that includes a man who, because of his celebrity status, abuses a child and gets away with it?

#2:   Yes, it does. But if it's any consolation, for all that walk, or buy their way out of trouble, at least three times the number are put away.

#1: That's not a consolation. Not in this case.

#2: That's because you're taking it too personally.

#1: And how am I supposed to take it?

#2: Like the professional that you are. You're new to this office. I guarantee this will happen again and if you can't accept that...the door's over there. I'd understand.

#1: Are you suggesting I quit?

#2: Not at all. A lot less sensitive lawyers than you have quit. I'm just saying that I'd understand if you don't think you can take the inevitable, and may I add frequent, disappointments.

#1: I don't quit! I just can't help but think that Kathy Jenner's going to regret this.

#2: Very possibly, but you have to let it go. If it's any consolation, this guy's life is probably ruined anyway. There's been too much press and too many unanswered questions. Let's just move on.

#1: *(Pause)* Fine.

#2: *(Takes a folder and gives it to #1.)* Here.

#1: What's this?

#2: Your new case. It's that guy who took those people in the bank hostage and killed the guard.

#1: Yeah, I know the case.

#2: It's pretty much a no-brainer.

#1: Really? How much money does this guy have?

#2: None.

#1: Fine then, I'll take it.

#2: Go home. I'll see you tomorrow. *(Exits.)*

(#1 sits back at his/her desk.)

34. The Child

(In a hotel room. #1 is pacing and waiting. He/she checks his/her watch. There is a knock at the door. #1 goes to the door, but doesn't open it.)

#1: Who's there?

#2: Joe/Jo, it's Bill/Barbara.

#1: Are you alone?

#2: Did you tell me to come alone?

#1: Just answer the question.

#2: *(Pause)* Yes, I'm alone. Let me in. *(#1 opens the door and let's #2 in. He/She looks around then sits.)* **Nice place. I think it has a minus four star rating.**

#1: Well, when one wants to be lost, one usually doesn't go to the Hilton.

#2: Where's Carrie?

#1: Not here.

#2: What is going on? You know she was supposed to be here.

#1: Wrong! On the phone you said you wanted to see me. Not the kid.

#2: I want to make sure she's OK.

#1: Give me a break. You know she's fine.

#2: Then why can't I see her?

#1: Because I don't trust you. You're my ex-wife/ex-husband's lawyer. For all I know, you brought the cops or the FBI with you.

#2: You're over-blowing your own importance, you know.

#1: And you're playing games with me, you know. Bye. *(Starts to exit.)*

#2: Wait...

#1: *(Turns back.)* No, you wait! You and that...person I was married to were the ones who went on the news and gave interviews. You said you just wanted to talk. Well, here I am, so talk!

#2: Helen/Howard wants Carrie back.

#1: You want to tell me something that most of the continental United States doesn't already know?

#2: We thought that if you were asked in person, you might give her back.

#1: Well think again.

#2: What do you hope to accomplish by doing this?

#1: How's being with my daughter for starters. Not being denied visitation.

#2: No one was denying you visitation.

#1: Really? What do you call one weekend a month and every other holiday?

#2: I call it the judgment the courts handed down.

#1: Do you call it fair?

#2: *(Pause)* It's the judgment of the courts.

#1: And it's garbage, so please spare me the rhetoric, counselor.

#2: And you think this is going to make things all better? When you get caught, and you will be, they'll never let you see her.

#1: OK, let's play this game. Let's say for the sake of argument, I give up. I take Carrie home, Helen/Howard and I make nice, what happens in a month? What happens with the new job?

#2: What job? What are you talking about?

#1: See, this is why we can't talk. You can't talk straight with me about anything.

#2: If you're referring to Helen's/Howard's new job... nothing is definite. It's...

#1: ENOUGH! Stop lying. Just once.

#2: *(Pause)* OK...he's/she's taking the job.

#1: 3,000 miles away?

#2: *(Pause)* Yes.

(The two just stare at each other.)

#1: You know, when Helen/Howard and I first talked about getting divorced, we agreed that we'd have joint custody. So I just couldn't figure out why he/she started fighting so hard for sole custody. Then a friend of mine, a detective, did some checking and we found out that he/she was offered a new position with her/his company ...across the country. Well, if we shared custody she/he knew I'd never agree to let Carrie move, so things started to make sense. Then, you entered the picture.

#2: You make it sound like a plot.

#1: Wasn't it? Once we got into court you took innuendo and turned it into fact, took personality traits and made them character flaws. In short, you pretty much made me about one step below Hitler. I wouldn't have given me custody based on what you said.

#2: I didn't make anything up! I don't set out to make villains, I...

#1: Of course you do. It's your nature. Lawyers like you have this inbred quality — very much like attack dogs. Nurtured correctly and pointed in the right direction, you'll destroy anyone.

#2: Was I the one who told you two to get married? Did I then make your marriage go sour? No. You two did that on your own. I was simply hired to do a job.

#1: And you did it extremely well.

#2: And if you're expecting me to apologize for that, well, don't hold your breath.

#1: And you don't care who you hurt, whose life you ruin.

#2: You want to give it a rest? There're no reporters or cameras here, so get off the soap box. I'm an attorney. My colleagues and I aren't angels of death. We just try cases. Know what I think? I think that if I had been your lawyer and things had turned out differently, we'd probably be having dinner right now and you'd be toasting my court-room expertise. You don't hate me, you hate what I did.

And the facts are, I don't hate you...I pity you because I'm forced to sit and listen to the rantings of a bitter man/woman who screwed up his/her own life and marriage and is trying to blame it on everyone else. Well, I'm not to blame. I just did my job...and did it well!

#1: Including making stories about my "problem"?

#2: Did you or did you not go into a treatment program?

#1: Three years ago after a knee operation, I had a slight problem getting off the pain killers. On my own volition, I went to a spa to get some therapy on my knee and clean out my system.

#2: This "spa" was a registered rehab center, was it not?

#1: Yes it was, but...

#2: That's all I said.

#1: Oh, come on, the way you told it I was on the streets knocking over liquor stores.

#2: Look, we can go all day saying who did what to whom, but it won't solve anything. The courts made their decision and as of right now you're a kidnapper. That's all anyone's going to see. Why don't you just give up?

#1: *(Pause)* Do you have any kids?

#2: No.

#1: Then you have no idea what it's like. The prospect of not being able to see your kid when you want.

#2: Even if you had joint custody, you wouldn't see her every day.

#1: You just don't get it. No I wouldn't have liked it, but a couple of miles away is liveable. Three thousand miles away is unacceptable and I won't have it.

#2: And what about Helen/Howard? Aren't you doing exactly to him/her what you say he/she did to you?

#1: You reap what you sow. If he/she hadn't tried to get everything his/her way, had she/he just been honest, we wouldn't be in this position, and that's the truth.

#2: So what are you going to do? You can't run forever.

#1: I can run as long as necessary. Don't underestimate me.

#2: Then don't be an idiot. We'll work something out. I promise.

#1: *(Laughs a bit.)* Let's just say your credibility is lacking. You go home, talk to that...him/her and I'll get in touch soon.

#2: When?

#1: Soon.

#2: She/he won't like this.

#1: Ask me if I care? You just tell him/her that he/she can... tell him/her I said "hi." Now get out.

#2: *(Starts to exit.)* I'll see you in court.

#1: Looking forward to it.

(#2 exits.)

35. The Client

(At a table in a restaurant. He/she is dressed pretty well, looking somewhat overdressed for where he/she is. He/she takes the last sip of a drink, then calls for a waiter.)

#1: **Excuse me.** *(Pause)* **Hey, waiter! My glass seems to be empty. You wanna do something about it?** *(#2 enters and goes up to the table ad looks at #1. #1 sees him/her.)* **You don't look like my waiter, but you'll do.** *(#1 hands waiter a glass. Waiter puts it back on the table and sits.)*

#2: **I've been looking for you everywhere. Where have you been?**

#1: *(Looks around.)* **My first guess would be...here. Then again, in my condition, I might be wrong. I could be there.**

#2: **Well, just for your information, there's a room full of people, not to mention about 15 senior partners who are expecting to see you tonight.**

#1: **Oh, come on. Do you really think that in a room of a hundred plus lawyers, one absent attorney is really going to be noticed?**

#2: **Ordinarily, no. But when said attorney also happens to be the guest of honor, his/her presence is usually expected. Don't you agree, counselor?**

#1: **Your Honor, I object to this line of questioning.**

#2: **On what grounds?**

#1: **On the ground that you're making too much sense and I'm in no mood.**

#2: **Objection overruled.**

#1: **It figures. This just isn't my day.**

#2: **It's not your day?! You were officially made a partner in the firm today. That's what the party is about. Remember?**

#1: **Oh, that's right.**

151

#2:   So back to the original question, what happened?

#1:   I'll take the fifth...or I'll take a fifth. I always get those two confused.

#2:   Come on, Mike/Michelle, what gives?

#1:   OK. *(Pause)* Does the name David Stewart mean anything to you?

#2:   No. Should it?

#1:   No, come to think of it, I guess not. That was before you joined our happy little firm.

#2:   Who's David Stewart?

#1:   He's a Beverly Hills yuppie, jerk I defended.

#2:   Sounds like a great guy.

#1:   He's a peach. One day this guy kicks the holy crap out of his wife, she has him arrested for assault and battery, he hires our firm, and I'm assigned to get him off.

#2:   Did you?

#1:   You bet. On a technicality nobody even remembered existed. I remember thinking what an awful person this guy is and I got him off. And the topper, he did everything he was accused of.

#2:   Couldn't you have refused the case?

#1:   Not if I wanted to move up in the firm of Lockwood, Fitzgerald, and Scott, I couldn't.

#2:   OK, I see where you're at. But this is hardly the first guilty scumbag that's ever walked before.

#1:   I know, but the story's not done yet.

#2:   What happened?

#1:   I was driving over to the banquet tonight and I got a call.

#2:   From Stewart?

#1:   The one and only.

#2:   Don't tell me, he did it again, right?

#1:   Wrong.

#2:   Well, that's...

#1: He killed her.

#2: He what?

#1: They were having an argument and he decided to cut it short by putting her head through the living room wall. Unfortunately, the human skull doesn't have the apparent rigidity of say...brick.

#2: Oh, god!

#1: So, I go down to the police station, Stewart tells me what happened and wants me to get him out. I told him I'd talk to the partners, I jumped in the car came here, and lived happily ever after.

#2: Have you told the partners?

#1: No. I was hoping they'd try and execute Stewart before I had to.

#2: Not likely. Look, tell them and have someone else assigned to the case.

#1: Can't do it. Stewart said he wanted me and no one else. If I refuse, he'll go to another firm.

#2: Let him go. The other partners will understand.

#1: They might if I worked for the firm of Easter Bunny, Santa Claus, & Tinkerbell.

#2: Maybe you're underestimating them.

#1: Look me in the eye and tell me you honestly believe that? *(#2 doesn't look at him.)* Yeah, I didn't think so.

#2: OK, you're right. They're going to want you to take the case. So take it. Figure out some way to get your mind around the moral ramifications, and defend this guy to the best of your ability. It's your job and it's what Stewart's entitled to.

#1: Says who?

#2: Says this little document called the Constitution. Maybe you've heard of it?

#1: I can't believe you just said that. This has nothing to do with Stewart's constitutional rights.

#2: The hell it doesn't. It's about his right to a fair trial and

153

competent counsel.

#1: And what about his wife's right to life, liberty, and...you know what, forget the other two. Let's just start with life. She's dead and he did it!

#2: And you're so sure he's going to get off.

#1: Yes.

#2: How do you know?

#1: Because he's got the best justice that money can buy and that's a fact.

#2: So refuse the case! Tell the partners you won't do it and take the consequences.

#1: But...

#2: But what? Moral indignation has its price? Yes, it does, but you can't have it both ways. You want to remain the golden boy/girl, then you do what they tell you and shut up. Otherwise, stand by your principles. They're admirable, but it very well may be costly. It's your call.

#1: You've got this party line down pretty well, don't you?

#2: Not at all. It's just that I can afford to be more objective.

#1: How come?

#2: Because I'm not in your place.

#1: Wanna trade?

#2: Not on a bet. I'd just as soon put off my "crisis of faith" for a while, thank you.

#1: Coward.

#2: And proud of it. Come on, let's go.

#1: Where to?

#2: The dinner. You really should go.

#1: What about Stewart?

#2: It's your night. He's in jail, what's he going to do? I think his...situation will hold until tomorrow morning.

(The two start to get up.)

#1: You're probably right.

#2: No counselor, I'm definitely right.

#1: *(Pause)* Boy, are you cocky.

#2: I know. I learned it from you.

#1: I'm not cocky.

#2: Oh, please, your picture's in the dictionary...

36. The Deal

(In the interview room of a police station or at a safe house. #1, a federal witness, is waiting. #2, a member of the DA's office enters. #2 spots #1.)

#2: Sit down.

#1: *(Turns and sees #2.)* **Williams, I'm surprised to see you. I thought I rated better than the DA's flunky.**

#2: **Like I said, sit down...and shut up!**
(They both sit.)

#1: **You really should be a lot nicer to me considering how important I've become lately.**

#2: **You're a criminal.**

#1: **But an important criminal. And I'm about to save the DA's political life.**

#2: **The only life you're saving is your own.**

#1: **Maybe, but a life is a life. As long as one gets saved what difference does it really make?**

#2: **Why don't we just do what we have to do. I don't want to be here any longer than necessary.** *(Pulls a pad out of his/her briefcase.)* **OK, let's take it from the top...**

#1: **Whoa. I believe we have some details to work out first.**

#2: **What are you talking about?**

#1: *(Gets up and starts to leave.)* **Look, when you and your boss want to stop messing around, let me know.**

#2: **Where do you think you're going?**

#1: **Back to my room.**

#2: **You walk out of here and the deal's off!**

#1: **What deal?! So far, there is no deal!**

#2: **Now who's messing around? The DAs offering immunity.**

#1: *(Comes back to his/her chair and sits down.)* **No, the DAs mentioned immunity, among other things, but I still don't see anything in writing.**

#2:   *(Pulls a document out of his/her case and hands it to #1.)* **Is this what you wanted?**

#1:   *(Looks over the document and tosses it back.)* **Not even close.**

#2:   **What are you trying to pull?**

#1:   **Obviously not as much as you. Look, if I give you Genovese you're going to have to do a lot better than just immunity from prosecution.**

#2:   **What do you want?**

#1:   **What I asked for.**

#2:   **Well, I don't know what that was, so why don't you enlighten me.**

#1:   **I do no jail time. I go into witness protection, I get relocated to a town of my choosing with a sizable bank account to start me off.**

#2:   **Is that all? Are you sure you don't want a national holiday named after you?**

#1:   **That's not a bad idea considering who I'm handing to you.**

#2:   **You're not handing us anybody.**

#1:   **I'm not?**

#2:   **Fine, you're turning over Genovese, but the only reason you're willing to give him up is that he's already put a contract out on you. See, word on the street is —you've already talked.** *(#1 doesn't respond.)* **What, no pithy witticism?**

#1:   **And I wonder who put that "word on the street"?**

#2:   **Got me. Maybe one of your buddies on the inside, maybe someone else. It really doesn't matter. All Genovese knows is that you're a bad risk now. And I think we both know what happens to bad risks. So, maybe you should stop making any demands and be happy we're willing to give you anything at all.**

#1:   *(Gets up and starts to pace.)* **Well, it does appear that the DA's office and the Feds have seemingly put me in a** precarious position...

#2: We had nothing to do with Genovese's contract...

#1: *(Cuts #2 off.)* Please, don't. It insults my intelligence and makes you come off as a complete idiot. What you all did was the smart move. Actually – I respect it, but ultimately it still comes down to one indisputable fact – I'm the only one you've got.

#2: There are others.

#1: If that were true, we wouldn't be talking. So, don't give me what I want, I'll go to jail, get very dead, and you'll have nothing. OR you can give me what I want and finally nail the most powerful crime boss in the country.

#2: You really think you've got it all figured out, don't you?

#1: I don't figure, I know.

#2: *(Pause)* Yeah, I suppose you do. You know what my truth is? I really don't care about any of you. In spite of all your supposed money and power, you're all two-bit hoods who would be doing everyone a favor if you'd simply wipe each other out. But since that probably won't happen, we'll take our victories where we can get them which means that you'll probably wind up getting exactly what you want.

#1: I know I will.

#2: But you're going to have to give us every detail. I want to know every meeting you and Genovese ever had. Who and what you talked about, what you were ordered to do, what you saw him do.

#1: Fine.

#2: And when we're satisfied that what you've given us is usable, then we'll finalize any deal. Got it!?

#1: Have you heard a word I said? You get nothing until my lawyer and I have a deal in writing.

#2: How do we know that anything you tell us can be used? That it's legitimate.

#1: Because you wouldn't have gone through all this if I

didn't have something.

#2: Don't be so sure.

#1: Oh, I am. You know, you, the DA, Genovese, you're all the same. You destroy to achieve what you want. But at least Genovese was up front about it. He takes care of his own problems. You all, on the other hand, don't have the guts to do it yourself. You couldn't get me on your own so you had to set me up.

#2: You're hardly an injured party.

#1: Never said I was. I'm just saying we're more honest about what we do. But you don't want to hear about that. So, if you want me, my knowledge of Genovese, my tapes...

#2: Wait a minute, what tapes?

#1: Oops. Did I forget to mention I recorded some of my conversations with Genovese?

#2: It's a fact that seems to have slipped by.

#1: Surprise. It's my ace in the hole and if you want to know more, I'll see you tomorrow.

#2: Why tomorrow?

#1: That'll give you time to get my lawyer here and draw up the agreement. Otherwise, don't come back. See, I'm tired and the game's over.

#2: And you think you won.

#1: Don't you know, we both won. *(Exits.)*

37. The End

(We are in a living room. #1 is laying back on the couch. There is a knock on the door.)

#2: *(Off-stage)* **It's me. Open up.**

#1: **It's open. Come in.** *(#2 enters and walks over to the couch.)* **Hi.**

#2: **Hi?! It's two o'clock in the morning and all you can say is, "Hi!"**

#1: **Well, I thought I'd start off with single words, see how it goes and work my way up to full sentences.** *(#2 is clearly not amused. Crosses to the door and starts to leave.)* **Where are you going?**

#2: **Home!**

#1: **No. Stay with me awhile.**

#2: *(Turns.)* **Why are you doing this to me?**

#1: **What?**

#2: **You call me up hysterical, and it turns out to be the same old stuff!**

#1: **Did it ever occur to you that I miss you and I'm not handling all this too well?**

#2: **That's not my problem.**

#1: **Then whose is it?**

#2: **Yours.**

#1: **I'm not the one who ran out on you.**

#2: **Oh, here we go again. We cannot keep doing repeat performances of this scene.**

#1: **Yes, we can because we haven't gotten it right.**

#2: **What haven't we gotten right? What haven't we discussed at least one hundred times?**

#1: **The why!**

#2: **No! We have discussed the why. You just refuse to accept it.**

#1: **Then explain it to me one more time.**

#2: What's the point?

#1: Because all you ever say is, "It wasn't working." That isn't good enough.

#2: Nothing will be. Tell me, what do you want me to say? You want a minute-by-minute analysis of our relationship?

#1: No! I just want to know how we can be together one day and not the next.

#2: It didn't happen overnight and you know it!

#1: Then how did it happen?

#2: I don't know! *(Pause)* Do you think everything was perfect between us?

#1: No. We had our problems. I know that, but I wouldn't give up on us without trying to save what we had.

#2: That's just it. We didn't have anything anymore. Why live like that? It was no good for me OR you.

#1: So you left for my own good. Thank you for being so unselfish.

#2: I didn't say that. I left for our own good.

#1: I still love you. Don't you love me?

#2: Stop! Don't do this.

#1: TELL ME!

#2: No! I don't ! *(Pause)* Not anymore.

#1: When did you stop?

#2: What difference does it make?

#1: I have to know.

#2: Fine. A year ago last July 18th. OK? Does that make it better now?

#1: Go to hell!

#2: *(Starts to exit, stops at the door and turns back to #1.)* You know, you're under some misconception that this is easy for me. What I did – was the hardest thing I've ever done in my life. When I started feeling it slip away, I did everything I could to stop it.

#1: Then why didn't you?

#2: Because a relationship is not like a cold. When it's not

> well you can't give it an aspirin and wait for it to get better.

#1: Then you should have talked to me then.

#2: I know that, but I wanted to make sure I knew what I felt before we discussed it. When I was sure, I did talk to you.

#1: You didn't talk. You left.

#2: I talked. But you didn't understand. No, you wouldn't understand.

#1: Oh, I understood. Look, I am not some obsessive psycho. Our relationship was very important to me and worth fighting for. Yes, you had problems with commitment, but it seemed like we we had gotten through those, so you'll excuse me if I was a little shocked when you bailed at the first difficulty.

#2: It wasn't the first difficulty and I didn't bail...

#1: Of course you did. Admit it.

#2: No! It was my longest relationship ever. So how dare you say I "just" bailed out. Maybe if you stepped back and took an honest look you'd see the real reason why you won't let go.

#1: And that is?

#2: You're relying on something that got comfortable and...and convenient. You were so content to always have someone to go to the movies with, or share the holidays with that you overlooked the fact that there was nothing else, anymore. I didn't want a drinking buddy anymore. I wanted to move forward and we weren't.

#1: *(Finally gets it. Pause)* I feel so stupid.

#2: Come on, don't say that...

#1: No, it's not me. It's you. We never had a chance.

#2: What are you talking about?

#1: If you see comfort and convenience as a detriment, then you're the one who doesn't get it.

#2: Meaning?

#1: Those are the best parts of being together. Not the movies or holidays, but the comfort of having someone there who'll listen to you. The convenience of being in love with your best friend. The comfort of knowing someone will hold you...just because, and the convenience of sharing your life. In the whole scheme, the rest is all garbage and you don't see that, do you?

#2:   I...don't agree.

#1:   Of course you don't.

#2:   If you're done, can I go now?

#1:   Yeah, you can.

#2:   *(Heads for the door, stops, but doesn't turn around.)* I do care about you, you know.

#1:   No, you don't. You care about you, and that's the real tragedy, isn't it?

(#2 exits. #1 watches.)

38. The Hit

(A Country/Western dance club. #1 is seated at a table. #2 enters, looks around, spots #1, goes to the table, and sits.)

#1: That seat is taken.

#2: I know.

(#2 takes a card, puts it on the table and slides it to #1, who looks at it and puts it away.)

#1: Did you have any trouble finding me?

#2: A little. You don't look like what I expected.

#1: You watch too many movies.

#2: Isn't this is an...odd place to meet.

#1: Yeah, well, anyone who knows me knows I hate this place, so people tend not to look for me here.

#2: I guess that makes sense.

#1: So I understand you have a "pebble in your shoe."

#2: Excuse me?

#1: You have a problem you want taken care of.

#2: Yes, I do.

#1: Tell me about it.

#2: I have a business. There are these...people who want to buy into the company. They could give more capital and probably help secure certain contracts.

#1: Sounds OK to me.

#2: But, I have a partner.

#1: Enter the problem.

#2: He doesn't want help from these people. He thinks they're scum...uh, no offense.

#1: None taken. So this partner of yours needs some... convincing. You want him talked to?

#2: That's already been done. He said he'd go to the police if he was bothered again. That's when...these people got me in contact with you.

#1: I see. *(Pause)* So, this pebble needs to be removed. **Permanently.**

#2: Unless you see any other way? Do you?

#1: Do you?

#2: I could try and buy him out, but I don't really have that kind of money and I don't think he'd do it.

#1: Then you've just asked and answered your own question.

#2: It just seems so...drastic. This person has been my friend and...

#1: Look, I'm not your conscience, or your mother. Right now you're wasting my time and you're ticking me off. *(Rises and starts to exit. #2 grabs his/her arm.)* Take your hand off of me!

#2: *(Recoils a bit.)* I'm sorry. Please don't go. I don't know what to do.

#1: *(Sits and leans in close.)* Let me make this as plain as I can for you. I'm a very black and white person. You have a problem. You want it taken care of. I'll do it. It's that simple. Now, you've got five seconds to tell me yes or no! *(Pause)* Time's up. Good-bye.

#2: Yes! I need it taken care of.
(They both sit back. There is a beat.)

#1: That's better. It'll cost you fifty. Twenty-five now. Twenty-five when it's done. *(#2 reaches into his/her pocket and pulls out an envelope. He/She slides it to #1. #1 picks it up looks in it and puts it away.)* Small bills. Looks like you had your mind made up a while ago.

#2: Do you think I'm happy about this?

#1: You think I care one way or another?
(There is a pause.)

#2: When?

#1: When what?

#2: When are you going to do this?

#1: The less you know the better.

#2: But...I don't know what I should do.

#1:   Nothing. You should do nothing.

#2:   Maybe I should take a vacation now.

#1:   Do you understand English? I said, do nothing! If you suddenly take off and your partner winds up — whatever, don't you think someone might take notice of that?

#2:   You worried someone might be able to trace it to you?

#1:   Me? I'm invisible. So is anyone who works for me. The only one who'll go down over this is you. And if you ever tried to implicate me or anyone else, there'd be no proof. But that doesn't really matter because you'd be gone before you ever got to trial.

#2:   Are you threatening me?

#1:   No, guaranteeing. Accidents happen in jail all the time. My employers have very long arms. Understand?

#2:   I understand that. What I don't understand is how all this got started. I worked very hard to get a business going and it's not fair that one person is stopping me from succeeding. Why should I have to go through all this to get what others have already got? How did things get so complicated?

#1:   I can't answer that. All I know is that you think you have a complicated problem and I know I have a simple solution.

#2:   You think that is a simple solution.

#1:   Yes I do. Sometimes it's the only solution. You just do everything as usual. I'll take care of the rest.

#2:   I'll try.

#1:   Don't try! Do it! Now, I usually don't do this, but I'll give you one last chance to back out. If you want I'll walk out, with the money I have. That'll be for my trouble and we'll pretend this never happened.

#2:   *(Pause)* How do I contact you to get you the rest of the money when the job's done?

#1:   *(Smiles at #2.)* You don't. After the job is done, you've got two days to get the rest to the Hotel Bradford. Leave it at the desk in a package for Mrs. Crawford. Got it?

#2:   Yes.

#1:   Two things. Don't take it yourself.

#2:   Why not?

#1:   You'll be watched. Second, don't think of stiffing me or my partners.

#2:   Was that statement for my own good, too?

#1:   Yours and your family's.

#2:   I get your message.

#1:   Good. *(Starts to rise and exit.)*

#2:   Can I ask you one question before you go?

#1:   What?

#2:   How do you live with yourself?

#1:   Very well. I don't plan these sort of things. People like you do. How are you going to live with yourself? *(#2 doesn't answer. #1 leans in close.)* Personally, I don't think you will, but that's your problem. Ciao. *(Exits.)*

#2:   *(Thinks for a second then turns.)* Wait...

     (#1 is no where to be seen. #2 turns back to the table and continues to drink his/her beer.)

39. The Homecoming

(In a house. #1 enters, looks around. #1 puts down a suitcase, then sits. #2 enters.)

#2: I see you finally made it.

#1: Yeah, I did. So what are you doing here?

#2: Your mother asked me to stay and help settle things.

#1: Well aren't you special.

#2: *(Checks his/her watch.)* Congratulations. It only took you fifteen seconds to become a jerk. Must be a new record.

#1: It's late. I don't want to get into this now. I'm here. Isn't that what matters?

#2: The funeral was yesterday. That's what mattered.

#1: Hey, I did the best I could! It wasn't possible to get here any sooner.

#2: Uh-huh. *(Turns and starts to exit.)*

#1: What do you know about it?

#2: I know that we've been trying to reach you ever since your father collapsed.

#1: I wasn't available. Maybe my father should have called to let me know he was planning to die. You know how he lived by his precious schedules.

#2: You always have an answer to everything, don't you?

#1: Pretty much, except I don't have the answer to what difference this makes to you. He wasn't even your father.

#2: It means a great deal to me. Your father...and mother, have been like parents to me for a long time. I'd do anything for them.

#1: So I've been told. So why do I have to even be here?

#2: Because he was your father...and your mother wanted you here. She thought the past should be forgotten now.

#1: Well, welcome to the real world. It's not! Just because someone dies doesn't erase what they've done.

#2: Can't you just do this for her? Do you always have to be so insensitive?

#1: Hey, I'm here, so you can shove your little insensitivity speech. And I'm here for my mother, but if you expect me to play the devastated, grieving child, forget it. The truth is, I don't feel that way and I won't pretend that I do.

#2: What was it between your father and you?

#1: None of your business.

#2: So you finally got back at him by missing his funeral, huh?

#1: It must be wonderful to live in your world where everything is so...simple. So black and white.

#2: It's not all black and white, but he was a good man and he deserved better than this.

#1: He was a "good man"?

#2: Yes, he was.

#1: Really?

#2: Really!

#1: To whom?

#2: Everyone.

#1: I would have settled for him being good to me.

#2: He was good to you.

#1: No, he was good to you and everyone else.

#2: And how was he so terrible?

#1: Don't put words in my mouth. I didn't say he was terrible.

#2: Then what was he?

#1: He was...nothing! He was absent. *(Pause)* He ignored me.

#2: I never saw that.

#1: Of course you didn't! Outwardly he was the perfect father, perfect husband. He had the act down to a tee.

#2: I don't understand. He always seemed very supportive. I know he was to me.

#1: You were his partner's child. You went into their business. So naturally he was interested in you.

169

#2: I don't believe he had no interest in you.

#1: Start! Look, I'm sorry if I'm ruining your image of him, but the facts are...nothing I ever did seemed to please him. Because what I wanted held no interest for him, I held no interest. Probably explains why I never liked you.

#2: Well maybe it's time you grew up. Nobody likes everything their parents do, but you're an adult now. If what you felt is true, just accept that and show him a little respect now that he's gone.

#1: Please. Spare me the sanctimonious speech, too. Listen to what I'm saying. I do accept the way he was. It took me a long time to put it in its proper place. I know I'm still somewhat bitter, but that's for me to deal with, not you. So don't you dare sit there and dictate to me that I should feel bad because I don't feel worse!

#2: OK, I've heard what you have to say and I think you had it pretty good. You know why I went into my father's business? I had no choice! The only reason I stayed was because of your dad! He was kind, supportive, tough and fair. So you'll excuse me if I don't see where you're coming from.

#1: That's fine! I'm not asking you to. I respect your opinion of my father, so please show me the same courtesy and respect mine.

#2: And you think missing his funeral was right?

#1: For me, yes.

#2: Why?

#1: Because I couldn't sit here and pretend during the service. Now I can go to the cemetery with my mother, I can help her settle things, do whatever she needs. But I don't have to put on an act and pretend to everyone that he was the perfect father. I think he'd even appreciate my not faking it.

#2: So this isn't just an act for attention?

#1: I'm an adult, you said so yourself. I don't do that. Not showing up yesterday was one of the hardest things I've ever done. But I had to be honest to myself.

#2: Did you even like your father?

#1: I didn't know him. It's like you might be with some distant relative of yours. Someone you might know of, but not know.

#2: I don't understand. You speak as if he wasn't even around. You grew up with him.

#1: No, I grew up next to him, not with him.

#2: You want to explain the difference?

#1: I can't. It's like they say about music, "if you can't feel it, I can't explain it." And trust me, you can't feel it.

#2: No, I guess I can't. I know my father wasn't the greatest either, but I can't imagine feeling nothing for him. Especially after he dies.

#1: What can I say? That's the way it is. I stopped trying to figure it out long ago. I've accepted it. So maybe you should just do the same. You just go on and grieve any way you want. I'm just asking you to let me be.

#2: If that's what you want...fine. I'll leave tomorrow and let you and your mom take care of the rest.

#1: Thanks. *(Pause)* I do appreciate you being here for her. Thank you for that, too.

#2: You're welcome. *(#2 starts to exit, but turns and starts to say something.)*

#1: *(Stops him/her.)* Don't! Just let it alone.
(#1 & #2 stare at each other for a second. Then #2 exits.)

40. The Interview

(In a county lock-up. #1, a reporter, is sitting at a table going over some notes. #2 enters. He/she is in handcuffs.)

#2: **Jack/Jackie King?**

#1: *(Looks up.)* **Yes.**

#2: *(Walks over to the table.)* **Thanks for coming.**

#1: **Why don't you sit down, Nancy/David.** *(#2 sits. #1 pulls out a mini tape recorder.)* **If you don't mind, I'm going to record our conversation.**

#2: **Go right ahead.**

#1: *(Starts the recorder.)* **Before we get started I have to ask you something. Why me?**

#2: **I saw you at the trial everyday and I've read your articles. You're a good reporter.**

#1: **Thank you.**

#2: **That's why I asked you to come here. I thought you'd give me a fair shot.**

#1: **Then let's get right to it. The jury only took four hours to find you guilty. Did that surprise you?**

#2: **Not really. A dozen people saw me shoot and kill Charles Armbruster. It's a little hard to fight evidence like that.**

#1: **Then what exactly do you hope to accomplish by having me interview you?**

#2: **I want people to know that I'm not a murderer.**

#1: **Let me get this straight. You waited for a cuffed and shackled, unarmed man to leave a court room. You went up to him and shot him three times at point-blank range. He was dead before he hit the floor, but you're not a murderer.**

#2: **No.**

#1: **Well, the state not only called it murder, they called it premeditated murder. So, I'd be interested in how you see it.**

#2: Charles Manson was a murderer. So was Jeffrey Dahmer. I shot an animal, a rapist. If it the was the Old West I would have probably been elected sheriff for what I did.

#1: Well, it isn't 1880 and this isn't Tombstone.

#2: *(Pause)* How much do you know about Charles Armbruster?

#1: *(Checks his/her notes.)* He was convicted of six felony assaults and rapes. Has been in jail more than he's been out...

#2: Did you know that the state classified him as a habitual criminal, but they still let him out? That he is the main suspect in seven other rapes in which two of the victims were killed, but was never brought up on charges because of lack of evidence?

#1: No, I didn't.

#2: We weren't allowed to bring any of that up at the trial. A human doesn't act like he did. I just put him out of everyone's misery.

#1: But according to the law the man had rights....

#2: Rights?! You wanna talk about rights? How about my sister's right? My sister was beautiful, talented, happy. That...he abducted my sister, raped her, beat the crap out of her and then dumped her body out of his van on the side of the road under the assumption she was dead.

#1: I know. I was at the trial. But she ID'd the van, picked Armbruster out of a line up. He was going to go to jail.

#2: So what? That's not good enough. Do you know he winked and smiled at my sister at the indictment? His going to jail wasn't going to start to pay back what he did to her.

#1: Did what you did to Armbruster heal her? Is she OK now?

#2: No. She...

#1: She's under a doctor's care and not doing well. *(Pause)* Yeah, I was at the trial. Remember? *(Pause)* Look, I can't start to imagine what she went through...or what your family is going through, but I can't condone vigilantism, either.

#2: It's not like I do this everyday to everyone...

#1: I didn't say you did, but do you know how many horrible crimes happen? To people just as innocent as your sister?

#2: I don't need a lesson on how bad society is.

#1: Maybe you do because you can't kill everyone who wrongs you. And I can't write an editorial on how your killing of a rapist is a good thing. You took another's life.

#2: And for all intents and purposes he took hers.

#1: *(Pause)* You're right, he did and now your family has to suffer two losses. Your sister's and yours. They all really need your support, but you won't be there to give it. Do you realize what you've done and where you're going?

#2: *(Pause)* Mr./Ms. King, Look at these... *(He/She holds out the cuffed wrists.)* I'm locked up and probably will be for a long time. I'm not a stupid man/woman. I'm going to jail, and for a long time, most likely. I am terrified of that and what might happen to me there. I may wind up dead. Who knows...but...

#1: But what?

#2: I take full responsibility for my actions and I'll take whatever the consequences are because in my heart of hearts, I don't believe I did anything wrong.

#1: *(Just looks at #2.)* I believe you and in a way I admire you. Still, I'm a reporter. I don't write an opinion column and I won't put my personal slant on the news. I just write it.

#2: So you're not going to interview me?

#1: I didn't say that. Right now, you're news. And an interview will sell papers. But we have to do it soon. The trial's over and the reality is, in a couple of weeks, nobody's going to remember you. Your fifteen minutes are up.

#2: That's a little cold.

#1: No, just the way it is. You should know that, but there are

> some ground rules.

#2: What?

#1: Like I said, I won't slant the story and I won't editorialize. I will try and get comments from the DA, the police, whoever I need to round out the story. This story won't be a soapbox for you. Can you live with that?

#2: I suppose.

#1: You'd better be sure, because it's not open for negotiation.

#2: *(Pause)* I just want to be heard.

#1: You will be. *(Turns off the recorder and starts to rise.)* I'll talk to my editor and make sure he wants to go with this. OK?

#2: Fine.

#1: *(Starts to exit.)* I will tell you something, off the record.

#2: What?

#1: If I had been in your place...I very well might be in your place.

#2: *(Starts to smile a bit.)* Thanks.

> *(#1 exits.)*

41. The Intimidation

(In an office. #1 is finishing up some work at his/her desk. #2 peeks his/her head in the door.)

#2: **Hey, you busy?**

#1: **I'm just finishing up some reports.**

#2: **Oh, sorry. I didn't mean to bother you.** *(Starts to exit.)*

#1: *(Stops her.)* **You weren't bothering me. What's up?**

#2: **Nothing, really.**

#1: **Are we still on for lunch?**

#2: **Actually, that's why I stopped in. Can I take a rain check for lunch?**

#1: **Sure. Anything wrong?**

#2: **No, I'm just...um...just...**

#1: **Just what?**

#2: **Not hungry.**

#1: **That would be a good reason.**

#2: **I've also got some reports of my own I should get done today. I'll talk to you later.** *(Starts to exit.)*

#1: **Whoa, hold on! Come in here.**

#2: **I really have a lot of work...**

#1: **Yeah, so you've said. Just get in here and close the door.** *(#2 comes all the way in and closes the door.)* **Sit down.** *(#2 pauses, then walks over to the chair by the desk and sits down.)* **So, you want to tell me about it?**

#2: **About what?**

#1: **I don't know, you tell me, but something's wrong.**

#2: **There's nothing to tell.**

#1: **Look Nancy/Nathan, I know you. You've barely said two words to anyone in the last week, and you've been disappearing right after work. So, again, what's up!?**

#2: **And I'll tell you again, nothing! OK? May I go now?**

#1: *(Pause)* **Fine. Whatever. Sorry I bothered you.**

#2: *(Starts to leave then stops. He/She keeps his/her back to #1.)* **Look, if I do tell you, will you promise me it won't leave this room?**

#1: **Do you really need to ask?**

#2: *(Turns and goes back to the chair and sits down.)* **OK...I... God, this is difficult.**

#1: **Just say it.**

#2: *(Pause)* **I'm being...bothered.**

#1: *(Pause)* **What do you mean, "bothered"?**

#2: **Intimidated.**

#1: **How?**

#2: *(Pause)* **Verbally.**
(There is silence.)

#1: **Are you going to tell me who it is and what's going on?**

#2: **I can, but it could put you in an awkward situation.**

#1: **You think I really care about that?**

#2: **You might.**

#1: **Tell me.**

#2: *(Pause)* **Bill Dodd.**

#1: **Bill!?**

#2: **See, what I mean?**

#1: **OK, start at the beginning and tell me everything.**

#2: **I guess it started right after I finished my orientation. Bill would drop by my office to find out how I was doing. Then he would drop "hints" that he didn't want me to have this job. That maybe I wasn't qualified.**

#1: **Go on.**

#2: **This went on for a few weeks, his visits became a little more frequent and his hints a little more clear.**

#1: **How "clear"?**

#2: **He said that he was the only one of the executives who voted against me for this job, and he felt I didn't know what I was doing.**

#1: **Do you know why he said all this?**

#2: **He finally spelled that out this morning. The final**

choices were me and his friend, Eric. He said Eric should be working here and he was going to quietly make sure that I didn't last.

#1: That's pretty...straightforward... *(Pause)* Why didn't you come to me with this before?

#2: Because at first...I though it would stop.

#1: But today, when it still hadn't, I had to practically brow beat it out of you.

#2: That's because it's a complicated situation. The man is Vice President. Also you recommended me for this job, and...and how would it look if after just a month I started something like this?

#1: How would it look? Who cares how it would look. And for your information, I recommended you for this job and you got it because you were the best person qualified. And as far as Bill Dodd goes, what he did is unacceptable.

#2: But he is your friend.

#1: So are most people who work here. That doesn't excuse what he did.

#2: So what do you suggest I do?

#1: As I see it, you have two choices. One; confront him. Tell him you're going to file a complaint.

#2: I don't know if I can do that.

#1: So, you'd rather do nothing?

#2: No, but it's his word against mine. Who's going to believe me?

#1: You said it yourself. You just started working here, you really have nothing to gain — so why lie?

#2: What's my other choice? You said I had two.

#1: You can quit.

#2: I don't want to quit.

#1: Then I stand corrected, you only have one choice.

#2: I could ignore the whole thing.

#1: You think that'll make him stop? Ignoring is not a choice.

#2: *(Pause)* All I wanted to do is work. I was so excited when I landed a job here. This really stinks.

#1: I agree. That's why you owe it to yourself to make sure this guy doesn't get away with it.

#2: And if I'm responsible for getting someone fired?

#1: If Bill gets fired, then it's what he deserves. Plus, you're not responsible for his actions. He is!

#2: I don't know if I can do this by myself.

#1: You won't have to. I'll go with you.

#2: But you just said that this is my problem.

#1: It is, but you don't have to solve it alone. I'm going in there with you.

#2: Are you sure you want to get involved?

#1: I'm already involved.

#2: *(Pause)* Thank you. *(Pause)* So when do we do this?

#1: Well, no time like the present.

#2: Now?

#1: Why? Should we wait until he intimidates everyone he doesn't like? Besides, you don't want to go to lunch.

#2: You know, now that you mention it, I think I'm getting hungry.

#1: Great, let's have Bill Dodd for lunch. I'm sure you'll find it satisfying.

#2: I hope so.

(The two get up and exit.)

42. The Killer

(In an apartment. There is a sheet covering a body on the couch in the middle of the room. The apartment is pretty much a mess. #1, a cop, is on the phone.)

#1: No, there's not much more to do here. **Forensics has done its preliminary and I'm just waiting for the coroner's van to get here. I'll be in as soon as they pick up the body.** *(Hangs up and heads into another room.)*

#2: *(Enters and looks around the room.)* **Well, someone needs to get a better maid service.** *(Goes to the couch and takes a peek under the sheet. #1 comes back into the room.)*

#1: **Put it down, Kelly!** *(This startles #2.)* **What are you doing in here? Don't you know what the tape on the door means?**

#2: **The glue didn't work?**

#1: **Cute. Always got a smart answer, don't you?**

#2: **I try.**

#1: **Well, answer this. You can leave now. There's nothing to report.**

#2: **Dead body on the couch, why don't I believe you?**

#1: **Because you're an incredible pain.**

#2: **Maybe, but I'd like to think of it as good reporting instincts. That's what made me decide to come over here this morning. Or was it the 700 cops outside not letting anyone in.**

#1: **So how did you get through?**

#2: **I know the manager of the building. I called her and she came down and let me in the back.**

#1: **I want to talk to her.**

#2: **After she let me in she went to find the guy in charge downstairs.**

#1: **Well, you're wasting your time here. It's nothing. A dead body in this city is hardly an unknown entity.**

#2: That's true except this one looks like it might be number fifteen.

#1: You're not gonna give me that "Tenement Terror" stuff, are you?

#2: It's not "stuff" and you know it!

#1: We've got some ladies that are being killed, I'll give you that. But you're the one who tagged it and made more of it than it is.

#2: Really? Who do you think I'm writing for? The Idiot Gazette? You've got fourteen, now fifteen, murders of women who appear to be in their twenties, done the same way, all in tenement buildings and you really want me to believe that it's random? And as far as the name goes...it sells papers.

#1: And that's the bottom line, right?

#2: Selling papers? Yeah, it is. Yours is to solve crimes and keep the peace and we both get paid for those bottom lines. Let's not make things out to be any more grandiose than that.

#1: I'm not being grandiose. Then again I'm also not causing a public panic by being irresponsible.

#2: Irresponsible? You tell me one fact that I've reported about this case that isn't true.

#1: It's not the facts you know. It's the facts you don't know that can hurt and are causing a panic.

#2: Fine, so fill me in. Let me know what's going on.

#1: At this point it's none of your business.

#2: Of course it's my business. It's every citizen in this city's business. We have a right to know!

#1: FACTS! Yes you have a right to know FACTS! Not speculation. That's the main difference between us. You can speculate on what's going on and report it. We can't. If we do...

#2: If you do...what?

#1: Someone innocent could get hurt or someone guilty

181

might go free. *(Pause)* There was a guy we picked up and questioned in a child molestation case about a year ago. It turned out he was perfectly innocent, but someone in the press got his name and...

#2: Wait, is that the guy who just sued your department...last week?

#1: Yeah, it is. He claims that because of all the notoriety, he was evicted, fired, and so on.

#2: I had nothing to do with that.

#1: I'm not saying you did, personally, but it was one of your colleagues. We didn't make a mistake by questioning someone. We had good reason, but you'd never know that now.

#2: You've got a point there, but this case is different.

#1: How?

#2: You know these murders are similar and they're happening in a specific area. So what else do you know? That's what the people around here have the right to know.

#1: Why, so that every tenant in every one of these buildings can report everyone they see that they don't know? Do you know how much manpower is wasted if we have to follow up every report?

#2: What if one of those reports is the guy you want?

#1: What if it's not?

#2: That's the chance you'll just have to take.

#1: No, that's the chance you're making us take. And unlike you, we don't have the luxury of being wrong.

#2: *(Pause)* No, I guess you don't.

#1: It's not just you press people. You happen to be the worst...

#2: Coming from you that's a compliment.

#1: Well, none intended. See, if you have a police chief who wants to be mayor, or a mayor who wants to be governor, or a governor who wants to be a senator, crap pours in from all sides. Then you wonderful people add your two cents in and a case like this gets raised to a much more dangerous level.

#2:   Why dangerous?

#1:   It gets done too quickly and carelessly. More people could get hurt.

#2:   You sound like you're saying you're in a no-win situation?

#1:   No, what I'm saying is this city is full of jerks who won't let us do our job our way. And again, present company included.

#2:   May I quote you on that?

#1:   Why ask, you will anyway.

#2:   True, very true. *(Starts to exit.)* I will tell you that you have given me something to think about.

#1:   So, you're not going to report this one.

#2:   Sure I am. That's front page news. But I'll try and avoid any...speculation. OK?

#1:   Whatever.

#2:   But if you get any solid leads, give me a call. Then I won't have to speculate.

#1:   *(Ponders this for a moment.)* We'll see. Now get out of here before I have you locked up for disturbing a crime scene.

#2:   Has anyone ever told you how pretty you are when you're gruff? The way your eyes twinkle...

#1:   *(Yells out.)* OFFICER! I need some assistance.

#2:   OK, I'm going. What a grouch. *(Pause)* Take it easy. *(Exits.)*

43. The Pay-Back

(#1 is on the phone in his/her office, late at night.)

#1: No. I'm going to be here for a while. *(Pause)* I don't know when I'll get home. *(Pause)* Yeah, I'll call you before I'm about to leave. *(Hangs up the phone and goes back to the computer on the desk.)*
(We hear a voice from the door.)

#2: My but aren't we a conscientious little worker.

#1: *(Jumps.)* Who is that!? *(#2 walks into the office. #1 sees who it is.)* You scared me.

#2: Relax. I was just in the neighborhood and I thought I'd pop up and say, "hi." *(Pause)* Hi. *(Sits in the chair in front of the desk.)*

#1: What are you doing here?

#2: I told you, I was just in the neighborhood. Besides, I was curious as to how the new job was going. *(Looks around.)* From the looks of things, I'd say things were going pretty well.

#1: If you're done, I think you know the way out.

#2: I don't know. It's pretty big. You wouldn't happen to have a map, would you? It's a little different from when it was my office.

#1: Get out!

#2: I don't think so. You and I need to have a little talk.

#1: No, we don't. I'm calling security. *(Picks up the phone and starts to dial.)*

#2: *(Pulls out a gun.)* Put down the phone.

#1: What... *(Looks up, sees the gun, and freezes.)*

#2: I said, put down the phone! Now!

#1: *(Slowly puts the phone down.)* What are you doing?

#2: What am I doing? *(Pause)* Let me tell you a little story. There's a person I know who, up to a little while ago, had a good job and was doing pretty well. Then in less than a month, that person is out of work, his/her reputation is shot, he/she can't pay the bills, and has no prospects. The funny thing is – that person didn't do anything wrong. So, what do you think about that?

#1: I don't know anything about it.

#2: You don't? Interesting. You know what's even funnier? You don't know anything about it, yet you wound up with that person's job. Coincidence?

#1: I got this job because I've worked my butt off and I deserve it!

#2: And landing the Roscoe Chemical account had nothing to do with it, right?

#1: I...um...see...no, you...

#2: You're stuttering. Why is that?

#1: I can't help it if the Roscoe people wanted to work with me and not you.

#2: That was my account. How did they even know about you?

#1: I don't know. Cheevers called me into his office and told me you were off the account and he was giving to me. That's the first time I ever saw the file.

#2: Now that's not entirely true, is it?

#1: Are you calling me a liar?

#2: I'm holding a gun. I can call you anything I want, but the facts are, you are a liar.

#1: Look I'm sorry you lost your job, but it's not my fault!

#2: OK, the truth. You came in here, when it was my office, photocopied my notes on the Roscoe account, and sold them to Ampex Chemical using my name. Then you told Cheevers that you had suspicions I was selling our clients' files. When it was confirmed, I was fired.

#1: You're demented! Why don't you get out of here before you find yourself in real trouble! I will call the police.

#2: *(Waves the gun.)* I don't think so.

185

#1: You're bluffing. Besides you can't prove any of this.

#2: I can't? You know, you may be bright, but you're not exactly clever. Do you think that none of this was traceable?

#1: You're fishing.

#2: I don't have to. It turns out that I have a friend at Ampex Chemical that I didn't even know I had.

#1: What are you talking about?

#2: Right before I got fired, I got a call at home from this guy who said that if I had anything else to sell, let him know.

#1: So, that doesn't prove it was me.

#2: Hold on, I'm not done. This guy said, he knew I couldn't talk long, but could he contact me at home or the other number I gave. I asked what number, and he gave me a cellular. I checked it against the office cellulars, and guess what? It was yours! Before I could say anything, I was fired. *(They just stare at each other.)* Nothing to say?

#1: What can I say. I did it.

#2: You wanna tell me why?

#1: Because this job should have been mine to begin with. I've been here longer and I'm every bit as good as you. Just because you had a friend on the board shouldn't have made any difference, but it did.

#2: I didn't get this job because of connections. I got it...

#1: Save it! You came in here demanding truth, well, try dispensing a little yourself. When you got this job, I did a little checking of my own. I saw the evaluation reports. We were dead even. The only advantage you had was a connection. Period!

#2: Would you have denied yourself a connection if you had one?

#1: I don't know, but let me ask you a question. What would you have done if you had been in my place?

#2: I wouldn't have destroyed another person's life. That's for sure.

#1: I had no other choice! I've been eating the dust of people like you for a long time. People I'm just as qualified as, or more. I'm sorry it had to turn out this way, but I had to think of me, not you!

#2: *(Moves forward to the desk.)* Well, you'd better start thinking of me, because right now, I'm your worst nightmare.

#1: And you think killing me will solve everything?

#2: I don't know about solving anything, but it will make me feel a whole lot better. But I don't think that'll be necessary.

#1: So what are you planning?

#2: *(Pulls out a letter.)* This is a confession. It outlines everything you did, in detail, and how you framed me.

#1: And if I don't do it?

#2: *(Goes for #1 and sticks the gun under his/her chin.)* Then this letter becomes a suicide note. Either way is fine with me. I'd prefer the confession, the alternative is just too messy.

#1: You'd never get away with this.

#2: Oh yeah, I would. I moved away, remember. No one knows I came to town or saw me come in here. I took a subway from the airport and by the time they find you, I'll be 2,000 miles away in my bed were I've been all night. So, don't even believe that I won't do it.

#1: Look, can't we just make a deal? I'll pay you. A lot. You can start over.

#2: Forget it! Sign.

#1: What about my life?

#2: I'll give you a quarter. You can call someone who cares. Sign! *(Puts the paper in front of #1 and pushes the gun deeper. #1 now picks up a pen and hesitantly signs the confession. #2 reads it, pulls the gun away and starts to exit.)*

#1: What makes you think I won't call the cops the minute you walk out of here?

#2: Because you're much smarter than that. You and I both know it. *(#2 exits.)*

44. The Problem

(In an office. #1 is packing up his/her personal things. #2 knocks.)

#1: Come on in. The morgue's open.

#2: *(Enters.)* I just heard. Tell me.

#1: What's to tell? I got called into the president's office, told what a disappointment I've become, and fired. Short and sweet.

#2: I'm sorry. I...

#1: Hey, it's not all bad news. I was given a whole hour to clear out my things. *(Goes back to packing.)*

#2: *(Starts to exit. Then turns back.)* What are you going to do?

#1: Go over my non-existent options, I guess.

#2: Look, I gotta tell you something.

#1: What?

#2: I knew this was coming down.

#1: *(Pause)* When did you find out?

#2: About a week ago.

#1: And you didn't tell me!? Terrific. Thanks for the support. Why don't you just get out of here.

#2: Look, I tried to talk to you.

#1: Really. Obviously you didn't try very hard since I don't remember.

#2: I'm not surprised you don't.

#1: What does that mean?

#2: Last week. After work at Antonio's.

#1: *(Starts to think.)* I don't remember you trying to talk to me.

#2: You were at the bar. I told you to come and sit down. That I wanted to discuss something with you.

#1: Oh come on, it was after work. I didn't want to talk about business. I was unwinding.

#2: Yeah, I know. You "unwind" quite a bit, don't you?

188

#1:   OK, you've obviously got something you want to get off your chest. So why don't you just say it?

#2:   Fine, have it your way. You're being fired because you have a problem. You're a drunk!

#1:   Who told you that? It's a lie!

#2:   It is? OK, you tell me. Why are you being fired? You're as smart as you were when you came here, aren't you? You're fully capable of doing your work, but you haven't been. Why is that?

#1:   You don't know what you're talking about. Roswell just doesn't like me. He never has. I...

#2:   Roswell likes you just fine. Or should I say liked you. He's just now seeing what everyone else already knows. You have a drinking problem and you can't do your job.

#1:   Get out of here! I really don't need this now.

#2:   Yes you do! Especially now. Look, I'm not saying this to you to throw salt in your wounds. We're friends, good friends and I want to help.

#1:   How? By walking in here on one of the worst days of my life and making up lies about me?

#2:   No, by coming in here and telling you what I know is true. I don't know who you think you're fooling, but it's not me. Or anyone else out there for that matter. You've been drinking today. I can smell it from here.

#1:   Of course I had a drink. I just got fired. What should I do? Go and have a cookie or...or an ice cream cone to celebrate?

#2:   OK, but what about yesterday or last week or last year. Every time you're in this office you're going to or coming back from getting a drink.

#1:   You're exaggerating.

#2:   Am I? Tell me, how long do you go between drinks?

#1:   A while.

#2:   A while? And how do you measure "a while"? In weeks...days...hours? By the way, sleeping doesn't

count. *(#1 says nothing.)* **Look, I'm not doing this because it's fun. You need help.**

#1: OK, I'm sorry if I'm coming off as difficult, but it's been a lousy day. Yes, I drink some, probably more than I should, but trust me I...

#1/#2: ...can handle it. *(#1 & #2 look at each other.)* No really, I can.

#2: You want to continue with this duet? I know all the verses.

#1: *(Looks at #2 then turns back to the packing. Softly)* I'm doing fine.

#2: *(Grabs #1 and turns him/her around.)* Doing fine!? Your packing up your belongings because you've just been fired! You call that doing fine!?

#1: *(Breaks free.)* What is all this to you? You wouldn't happen to be worried that my being fired is going to reflect badly on you. After all, weren't you the one who brought me in here?

#2: No, I'm not worried at all because when you came here you were doing great. I didn't know you had a drinking problem until later.

#1: And why are you so sure that I have a problem?

#2: Because I've been there, I've done it, and... *(#2 reaches into his/her pocket pulls out a chip, and tosses it to #1.)* I've got the chip.

#1: You're...

#2: Sober. Six years now.

#1: I...I didn't know.

#2: I hit bottom a couple of years before we met.

#1: You really haven't had a drink in six years?

#2: No, I really haven't.

#1: I guess you don't want one.

#2: Only all the time.

#1: How do you...not drink?

#2: One day at a time. Today's easy though.

#1: Why?

#2: All I have to do is look at you...packing.

#1: *(Tosses the chip back.)* That's not fair!

#2: Neither is being a drunk. And if you don't get some help, and fast, this is going to become a very familiar scenario for you. I can guarantee it.

#1: Not very compassionate, are you?

#2: Oh, I've got a lot of compassion, but for someone who's truthful with themselves. I can't afford to indulge a lie, and know what? Neither can you. And right now, you are living a lie.

#1: You don't know anything about me! Yeah, we're friends, but you don't know all the pressure I have. Home isn't great, I have to compete all the time at work, I can never relax. Do you know what that can do to someone? Do you know how all this makes me feel about me?

#2: Probably not too highly considering how much time you spend in altered states. But the thing is, and listen carefully, it can change! But you have to want it to.

#1: Don't you think I want it to?! Don't you think I'd love to leap out of bed and look forward to the day? I just need time to straighten things out, and I can do it on my own without you or your meetings.

#2: Who knows, maybe you can. Being unemployed will certainly give you the time to find out. *(Takes a card out of his/her pocket and hands it to #1.)* Even so, you might want to stop by a meeting sometime. There are only about 1500 meetings a week. See if you can squeeze one in. Who knows, maybe we can learn a thing or two from you. *(Starts to exit and turns back.)*

#1: I'll get a handle on this. I'll be fine.

#2: Well, you've got our number and believe me...we've got yours. See you. *(Exits.)*

191

45. The Prosecutor

(In the District Attorney's office. #1 is in a conference room going over a file. #2 enters.)

#2: I assume there's a good reason for calling me in on a Saturday.

#1: Why, did I take you from something?

#2: Nothing big, just my private life.

#1: You work for the DA. You don't have a private life.

#2: I keep forgetting that.

#1: Don't worry, we'll make it up to you.

#2: When?

#1: Uh...let's see...never.

#2: Sounds fair.

#1: Look, I'm sorry, but I got called in on this, too. I was told it couldn't wait till Monday.

#2: So — what's up?

#1: Ever heard of Franklin Marshall?

#2: The oil guy?

#1: That's the one.

#2: Didn't he just die or something?

#1: Not "or something." He's very dead.

#2: And what, an autopsy come back with results that turned out to be suspicious?

#1: Why did you say that?

#2: Because anytime one of these guys who has more money than God, dies in this town, the autopsy's almost always suspicious...to someone. Anyway, I heard this guy had about ninety different types of cancer. All fatal.

#1: He did, but that's only part of it.

#2: So, give me the front page.

#1: OK, we got an eighty year old, almost billionaire, who dies, leaving behind a daughter and a wife.

#2:   What number wife?

#1:   Four.

#2:   Is she young?

#1:   That's a rhetorical question, isn't it?

#2:   Mostly. How young?

#1:   Twenty-five.

#2:   Ouch!

#1:   Anyway, little Miss twenty-five informs the police that according to the old man's doctors, he wasn't supposed to die yet and she wants an autopsy.

#2:   OK, so far so ugly, and the autopsy shows...

#1:   The autopsy shows some drugs. When the police tell this to the grieving widow, she drops the news on them that the daughter was with him, alone, when he died.

#2:   Oh, I was wrong, this isn't ugly, it's...

#1:   Really ugly? But wait, it gets better. The cops talk to the daughter. And she tells them, yes, she was with her father. He said he was in incredible amounts of pain and could she get him his pills. She did. Then she filled a glass of water, he took the pills, and then he died. *(Hands the folder to #2.)*

#2:   *(Opens it and starts to read.)* It sounds like a bad soap opera.

#1:   Well, here's the kicker. The DA wants to charge the daughter.

#2:   With what?

#1:   Maybe assisting a suicide.

#2:   *(Pause)* He's nuts. It'll never fly.

#1:   Why?

#2:   Big reason – no motive. *(Indicates folder.)* It says here, daughter and stepmom will get about 400 million apiece. That would be a motive if it wasn't for the fact that the daughter is president of the old man's company and pulling in a seven figure salary. He wasn't long for this world anyway, so why hurry along the inevitable? Plus

193

the autopsy is inconclusive. The drugs found were his prescription.

#1: So why do you think stepmom is pursuing this?

#2: She probably wants a little more of the pie and is trying to cause trouble. Nothing more. My opinion is that we should walk away from this one. *(Hands the folder back.)*

#1: Well thanks for your opinion, but we didn't call you in for that. The DAs going ahead with this and he wants you to prosecute.

#2: Well, good for him. That makes one of us.

#1: What are you saying?

#2: I'm saying, forget it. No way! This case is a loser.

#1: Well the DA doesn't agree with you. He's got a bug about this case and he wants it prosecuted.

#2: Then let him do it. Oh, I forgot, the man hasn't walked into a courtroom since Lincoln was president. Look, he's got a thousand lawyers in this office. Can't he get one of them?

#1: No, he wants you.

#2: Why?

#1: He said he likes your courtroom flair. He also feels this case is similar to the Perez case. You won that one big.

#2: This is nothing like the Perez case. Those kids hired someone to shoot their parents for their inheritance.

#1: And you don't think the two have any similarities?

#2: None. Also, we're going to get into issues like assisted suicide, the right to die with dignity, things that'll keep this case going for months and they're obviously not true. It'll...*(Just stops talking.)*

#1: What?

#2: I'm so stupid. I know why he's so hot on this. It's an election year. He's hoping this high-profile case will stay hot right through election day. He'll then be the DA who is tough on the rich and the poor.

#1: Wait, you're blowing this...

#2: And I'm the flavor of the month. I won the Perez case and the media really likes me. *(Pause)* Tell me I'm wrong.

#1: I can't, but I can't say you're 100% right either.

#2: And you know what else, if this does go past election day, the outcome won't mean a thing. We'll put that woman through a lot of grief needlessly, waste months of my time and a lot of taxpayer money on a case that's unwinnable.

#1: You sound pretty sure of yourself.

#2: I'm very sure of myself.

#1: Good, because if I tell this to the boss, you probably won't have to worry about this case...or any others, for that matter. You know how he is. He doesn't like people who think they're smarter than him.

#2: Then he must hate everyone.

#1: If you dislike him so much, why are you here?

#2: Because I like being a prosecutor. I didn't vote for this guy and if the word on the street is correct, he won't be here that much longer. Besides, he'll never get rid of me.

#1: Can you afford to take that chance?

#2: It's not chancey. For one, I am popular with the press. He needs me, and two; if he does fire me, I've been made a book offer on the Perez case that'll tide me over nicely until he's out of office. I really can't lose.

#1: You want me to tell him that?

#2: Just tell him I won't take the case, and he shouldn't either. Then whatever happens, happens.

#1: I'd really hate to see you leave.

#2: I'd hate to see me leave, too, but I will. I feel that strongly about this.

#1: I believe you. *(Pause)* OK, I'll relay your message.

#2: *(Starts to exit.)* See you Monday...I hope.

#1: Me, too.

(#2 exits.)

46. The Retirement

(In the coffee room of an office. #1 is on the phone as he/she pours some coffee.)

#1: Yes, I know. You're not giving me any new news here. *(Pause)* I know he didn't show up. *(Pause)* What? No, don't put him on hold. Transfer the call here. *(#2 enters. He/she goes up to #1 and starts to say something. #1 holds up a hand. Then talks into the phone.)* Burt, yes I know how long you've been waiting. *(Pause)* No, he was on his way over and his car broke down. *(Pause)* Because he left his cellular on his desk. He hates that thing. You know how my dad is. *(Pause)* I know it's not the first time. Look, John Alexander is on his way with the new contracts. He should be there in five minutes. I promise. *(Pause)* I'm glad I could help and I owe you a drink. *(Pause)* No, you tell my Dad that. He doesn't let me use that kind of language. *(Pause)* You, too. Good-bye.

#2: Nice save.

#1: It helped that my father and Burt Goldman have known each other for thirty years. So, have you seen my dad?

#2: He's in his office. He's saying that he wasn't informed of the meeting.

#1: Uh-huh.

#2: Do you want me to talk to him?

#1: Is he yelling at everyone?

#2: Of course.

#1: No, let him alone. He's mad at himself. He needs time to cool down. I'll talk to him later.

#2: Whatever you say. *(Starts to exit, then turns back to #1.)* You know this is getting worse, don't you?

#1: I don't want to talk about it. *(Picks up a newspaper and starts to read.)*

#2: *(Walks back to #1.)* We have to.

196

#1:   No, we don't. There's nothing to discuss. My father is fine.

#2:   Yeah, and our company tops the Fortune 500 list. Look, there's no one I love more than the old man, but facts are facts. He really can't do his full job anymore.

#1:   That's not true. He's still the best at what he does.

#2:   True...when he's aware...or remembers. *(Pause)* Everyone knows his memory's no good now and...

#1:   Who did you tell!?

#2:   No one and I'm insulted you think I told anyone. You don't have to attend Harvard Medical school to figure out that there's a problem.

#1:   What's everyone saying?

#2:   The truth. That when he's aware he's fine, but he forgets too much, repeats himself too much.

#1:   So you're saying that nobody trusts him?

#2:   I'm not sure if trust is the right word, but in a nutshell... yeah. It's real hard to sit in a meeting and watch him ask questions that were answered twenty minutes before...or walk in on a meeting having no idea he was supposed to be there...or...

#1:   Or...forgetting a Burt Goldman meeting for the third time. Yeah, I get the point. *(Pause)* Have you heard if anyone on the board knows? *(#2 doesn't answer.)* Your lack of an answer doesn't bode well for my father.

#2:   I don't know anything definitive, but the talk is...they're planning to have a meeting about asking your dad to step down.

#1:   What? Why hasn't anyone talked to me about it? This is inexcusable...

#2:   Whoa, you wanna get a grip? I said it was just a rumor.

#1:   But what if it's true?

#2:   OK, what if it is? If they are planning to replace the old man, you're not exactly the first one they'll come to for support. Also, if they are holding this meeting, can you honestly blame them?

#1:   He started this company.

#2:   I didn't ask that. Can you blame them for thinking your dad should step down?!

#1:   *(Pauses, then quietly.)* No. *(Pause)* I went with him to see his doctor a little while ago. The doctor wanted to put him on some medication.

#2:   But your dad didn't want any part of it. And I bet he was very demure in his objections.

#1:   He's getting much better. He didn't go ballistic until the third word left the doctor's mouth. Still, he's not an invalid, so why shouldn't he work?

#2:   Hey, he's seventy. Most people are retired at that age. He's done a great job. He created this company and made it work. He doesn't have to give it up. Maybe he could be in an advisory position. But now's the time to sit back and enjoy life while he can.

#1:   Enjoy life? That's funny.

#2:   Why?

#1:   Because this place is his life. Get it? It's what he loves. Now don't get me wrong, I'm not going to be one of those people who say they never saw their father. I mean, he loved his family, but his work...I don't know. Maybe it's the way he used to walk out of the house in the morning. He just loved going to work. It's always given him something...I just can't describe.

#2:   Think of your dad back then. How would he judge his performance now?

#1:   He wouldn't like it.

#2:   Then convince him to go out on top. Not like a ballplayer who sticks around too long and can't contribute. Someone who can't be productive.

#1:   Sorry. Maybe the board should do it because I won't.

#2:   Why not?

#1:   Because I can't. Good enough?

#2:   Not even close. Don't you care about the business?

#1: I care about him more.

#2: Then you owe it to him to be honest. If you ask, he'll probably step down.

#1: Exactly!

#2: Exactly, what?

#1: If I ask him, he will step down. He'll argue, eventually listen to me and retire. But I won't be the one to take this away from him. *(Pause)* I won't kill him.

#2: Maybe he wants to step down.

#1: Shortly after my Uncle Joe retired, my dad and I went to visit him. We spent the day going to the park, etc. Anyway, on the way home my father wasn't talking. I asked him if he was OK and he said, "If I ever say I want to retire, just shoot me right there. When I go, it's going to be at my desk with my pen in my hand."

#2: Was that before or after his current problem?

#1: Before.

#2: Things are different. Your dad may not always be aware, but he's not oblivious. Maybe he's waiting for someone he loves to tell him it's OK to stop now.

#1: In the movies, that would be the ending. But unfortunately this isn't Hollywood and he's not sweet, old Jimmy Stewart. It's not a very realistic hope.

#2: If you don't talk to him, you'll never know.

#1: I need to think about this.

#2: Don't take too much time. If the rumors are true, this whole conversation will be moot in about three days. It's your call. *(Gets up and exits.)*

#1: *(Watches him/her go, then pauses. Softly)* **Why?**

47. The Set-Up

(In an office of a large advertising agency. #1, an ad executive, is on the phone. During the course of the conversation #2 enters.)

#1: Harold, you want to relax? I told you yesterday that it was just a preliminary campaign strategy, didn't I? *(Pause)* Yes, of course I have some other ideas. *(Pause)* No, you can't have them this afternoon. *(Pause)* Because they're not fully written out. *(Pause)* Tomorrow...afternoon. *(Pause)* Have we ever let you down? *(Pause)* I'll talk to you tomorrow, Harold. Good-bye. *(Hangs up.)*

#2: That's was some pretty good tap dancing. Mr. Bo Jangles would have been proud.

#1: Do you have something relevant to say, or do you just get off lurking in other people's doorways?

#2: Actually, I was coming to tell you that Harold McBride has been trying to reach you, but I see that he got hold of you. He seems...upset.

#1: It was nothing serious. Harold's just the excitable type.

#2: Funny, he wasn't when Marsha was his account executive.

#1: That's because she never gave him any ideas that were worth getting excited about. That's why I handle his advertising now.

#2: Is that why?

#1: What do you want?

#2: Aside from Harold's message, we're having an accounts meeting at two.

#1: Sorry, can't be there.

#2: "Can't be there"? This isn't a request. All account executives are expected to be at the meeting. Mr. Lawrence's orders.

#1: Well, I'm not like the rest of the account executives, am I?

#2: What makes you so cocky?

#1: Why is it that when someone has some guts, they're referred to as "cocky" in that derogatory fashion?

#2: Cocky's not always derogatory. It's a compliment to some people. Not you of course, but to some people.

#1: I'm pretty sure you used to like me, didn't you?

#2: Like you? I hired you.

#1: Then what happened? I moved up the ladder too fast for you? You uncomfortable now that we're equals?

#2: No, you've just got a little too...slick. Let it go at that, OK?

#1: I don't think so. Why don't you like me?

#2: Because you want to get by on a pass.

#1: Meaning what, exactly?

#2: You've just horned in on everyone else's accounts.

#1: That's simply not true.

#2: Really. Harold McBride and McBride Toys used to be Marsha's account. Southeast Airlines, used to be Bob's, Chunky Cookies used to be David's. Need I go on?

#1: Is it my fault I came up with some fresh new ideas for these accounts and Mr. Lawrence turned them over to me?

#2: Not if the ideas were actually yours.

#1: Are you insinuating that I stole my ideas?

#2: There are some who believe you did.

#1: Well, they're wrong! I'm just one step ahead.

#2: If you say so.

#1: You don't believe me?

#2: I figure it's best to stay out of it. *(Starts to exit.)* By the way, just so Mr. Lawrence doesn't think you're off playing golf or something, why won't you be at the two o'clock meeting?

#1: Contrary to popular belief, I'm securing a new account.

#2: Really? Who?

#1: I'd rather not say.

#2: Come on. I thought we were on the same team. We don't

steal around here. Remember?

#1: Have you ever heard of Harper Electronics?

#2: Harper Electronics. Someone just mentioned them. *(Pause)* I know, Gail said something about them at lunch the other day.

#1: Really, well, I've researched them and it seems that they're a rising computer company. So, I got to their VP of advertising and it looks like we'll be handling them. I have the preliminary contracts right here. *(Shows #2 a large envelope.)*

#2: Well, it sounds like you got really lucky.

#1: Luck had nothing to do with it.

#2: That's good, because luck does have this funny way of running out. Anyway, I've got to get back to work. *(Starts to leave, but turns back.)* Oh, since you won't be at the meeting, you want to sign this for Mr. Lawrence? *(Takes out a letter and brings it over to #1 and puts it in front of him/her.)*

#1: What is it?

#2: A resignation letter. Yours to be exact. Effective immediately.

#1: *(Drops his/her pen.)* Whoa, did I just miss something in the last ten seconds? Who the hell said I was resigning?

#2: I did.

#1: And why would I do that? *(#2 pulls a Polaroid picture out of his/he pocket and gives it to #1.)* Wait a minute. This is...

#2: Bill Conrad. VP of Harper Electronics. Also... my brother-in-law.

#1: I...don't understand.

#2: I can see that. Let me explain. Some of your fellow employees came to me saying they thought you were going through their desks...

#1: Wait, that's not...

#2: Hold on. Now, none of them had any proof. I had my own suspicions, but like them, I had no proof, either. So we decided to get some.

#1: You set me up?

#2: Exactly. We created a company, got it a voice mailbox, talked a lot about it around the office, left a file about it with the name of the VP of advertising in my desk then you and nature ran its course. My brother-in-law was happy to do me a favor and play the VP.

#1: That doesn't prove anything.

#2: Give it up. The minute you called the number proved you went into my desk. Because that's the only place it was. We went through with the meeting because I wanted concrete proof. And we got that with your signature.

#1: What do you want?

#2: I told you, you're out of here. The letter says you've been offered another job and you're taking it.

#1: Why don't you just tell Lawrence what happened?

#2: Bottom line, I just want you out. I'm not out to ruin anyone's life. Not even yours. Believe it or not, I think you're good at advertising. After you steal someone else's client, that is. Who knows, maybe you'll learn something and clean up your act. I doubt it, but maybe. And if you don't, you can ruin someone else's company.

#1: I can fight this and you know it.

#2: No you can't and you know it. So why don't you just ooze on out of here like the scum that you are before I forget I'm a nice person. OK? *(Starts to exit and turns back.)* You'll forgive us for not getting you a going-away gift, but you understand. *(Exits.)*

48. The Suspect

(Cop #1 is seated at a table in an interrogation room. There is a knock on the door. #2 enters. #1 looks up.)

#1: Mr./Ms. Hansen. Thank you for coming in. I hope you haven't been waiting too long.

#2: Not at all, Detective...

#1: Dickerson. Please, sit down.

#2: *(Sits.)* You wouldn't mind telling me what this is all about, would you? Your message didn't say much.

#1: I didn't want to alarm you on the phone.

#2: But it's OK in private. Fine, I'm alarmed. Why am I here?

#1: It's about your father.

#2: My father's dead.

#1: I know, but we just received his autopsy report and...

#2: Autopsy? Why was an autopsy done? His doctor said it was a heart attack.

#1: I know, but when a relatively healthy man dies from a heart attack in a hotel room...the police usually want to check it out. Anyway, that's what the Chicago police did before they shipped his body back here.

#2: Detective, my father wasn't a young man.

#1: He wasn't extremely old either. Let me ask you, did he have a history of heart problems?

#2: Not that I know of.

#1: And his doctor didn't know of any, so there's our problem.

#2: You've lost me. What problem?

#1: *(Opens a folder and looks at the top sheet.)* It appears that during the autopsy, traces of a heart drug were found. This particular drug is used to stabilize an irregular heartbeat. Problem is, in a healthy person, this drug could actually cause a heart attack. Now, if you father had no problems, why would this drug be present?

(Pause) **Any thoughts?**

#2: *(Stares at #1.)* **Absolutely none.**

#1: **That's too bad. I was hoping you could shed some light on this.**

#2: **Well, I'm sorry. I can't.** *(Starts to get up to leave.)*

#1: **You didn't get along too well with your father, did you?**

#2: **You know who my father was, don't you?**

#1: **Everyone knows who your father was. Why?**

#2: **Because it sounds to me like you're trying to create something that isn't there. Maybe generate a little publicity for yourself along the way.**

#1: **Is that what it sounds like to you?**

#2: **Yes, it does.** *(Pause)* **Should I have a lawyer here?**

#1: **Do you need a lawyer here?**

#2: **I didn't think so until you started this line of questioning.**

#1: **What line of questioning? All I asked was if you got along with your father. And you know, you still haven't answered me.**

#2: **We got along fine!**

#1: **Really? Your business partners don't think so.**

#2: **Look, my father had definite ideas on how our business should be run. A lot of times we had...words over those ideas. It's natural in business.**

#1: **I wouldn't know. I'm just a cop, but what I do know is now that he's gone, you're the boss.**

#2: **As it should be. I was the next in line. OK? Are we done?**

#1: **Just one more question.** *(Picks up a photograph and takes it over to #2.)* **Do you know this man?**

#2: *(Looks at the photo.)* **It's Joseph Chambers.** *(Hands the photo back.)*

#1: **He worked for you, didn't he?**

#2: *(Pause)* **He worked for the company. My father fired him.**

#1: **When?**

#2: **About a year and a half ago, I guess.**

#1:   When's the last time you saw him?

#2:   I don't know. I assume around the time he was fired.

#1:   Do you know where he is now?

#2:   No and I really don't care.

#1:   Well, let me fill you in. He's in a jail cell downstairs. A chambermaid at the hotel in Chicago thought she saw him coming out of your father's room. When your father turned up dead, they dusted his room and Chambers' fingerprints were on the door knob. He was arrested at his apartment here a few hours ago. Know what we found in his apartment?

#2:   Let me guess, heart medicine?

#1:   Bingo!

#2:   Well congratulations. You cracked the case.

#1:   You don't seem to terribly broken up by the whole thing.

#2:   Look, detective, you were right about something. My father and I were not the best of friends. Then again, he wasn't friends with many people. He used to say he wouldn't be surprised if one day he were killed by a business associate, competitor, or an ex-wife. He had five, you know. So, I'm not really surprised how his life ended.

#1:   And you haven't seen Joseph Chambers in over a year?

#2:   I told you I haven't. Are you implying that I had something to do with...this?

#1:   Let me put it this way, you did have the most to gain.

#2:   You're deluded, not to mention treading dangerously close to libel. You have Chambers in custody, what more do you want?

#1:   The one who planned this because I have more than a hunch that Chambers didn't. *(Takes a phone bill out of the folder and puts it in front of #2.)* See the highlighted number? Someone called Chambers from your office around six o'clock the day before your father went to Chicago.

#2:   *(Looks at the bill.)* Correction. Someone called Chambers from the switchboard. There are over 1500 people working in that building. Any of which could have stayed late and called. Now, do you have anything else? *(A silence.)* I didn't think so. Good evening, detective. *(Starts to leave.)*

#1: You're pretty sure of yourself, aren't you?

#2: Not really. I just know what I did and didn't do. Also, if my father taught me anything, it was not to be intimidated by people who are beneath me and not half as smart as I am.

#1: Really, well, smart people make a lot of mistakes, too.

#2: Not in my case. Anyway, you want to take a shot at me, fine, go ahead. But when you miss, and you will, you're going to fall, and fall hard.

#1: Mr./Ms. Hansen, when I take a shot, I never miss and if I choose to come after you, you'll be the one falling. I guarantee it.

#2: *(Pulls a business card from his/her pocket.)* If you need anything else, call my attorney.

#1: Had that card all ready for me, didn't you?

#2: I'm always ready.

#1: We'll see. You can go.

#2: I know.

(They stare at each other for a moment. #2 exits.)

49. The Termination

(In an office. #1 is at his/her desk looking at a file. He/she is not very happy with it. #2 knocks on the door and looks in.)

#2: Hey, I'm heading out to lunch. Want to go with me?

#1: I can't, but come on in. I need to talk to you.

#2: OK. *(Enters and goes to the desk and sits.)* What can I do for you?

#1: Take a look at this. *(Hands #2 a folder.)*

#2: *(Flips through it.)* It's my analysis of the proposed buyout of Mitchell Industries.

#1: I know. Now, check it carefully and see if you see anything wrong.

#2: I checked this three times before I handed it in.

#1: Just humor me and check it again.

#2: *(Starts to look through it again.)* It looks fine.

#1: OK, now take a look at the report summary sheet. *(Hands #2 another piece of paper.)*

#2: *(Looks it over, sees something and stops. Quietly)* Oh no.

#1: You wanna tell me how this happened?

#2: I...I don't have an answer.

#1: I'll tell you, you better do better than that. When you analyze a company and figure its purchase price to be seventy million, but in your summary report that figure winds up reading one hundred and seventy million, well, I'm afraid that "I don't have an answer" just won't cut it.

#2: I obviously added a one. It was an honest mistake.

#1: Unfortunately the ramifications of a mistake of this caliber, honest or otherwise, can be pretty enormous... and costly.

#2: OK, I understand that, but...

#1: But, what?

#2: Couldn't they have just looked at the full report?

#1:   Let me explain how things work.

#2:   I know how things work.

#1:   Obviously, you don't. When the CEO and his top guys decided they want to buy, they had a list of companies that were ripe for a takeover. They then gave their vice presidents, one of which was Farady, a couple of companies to analyze, Faraday in turn gave me Mitchell Industries, which I turned over to you. When done, the report goes back up the ladder to the top.

#2:   OK, but neither of you looked at the report.

#1:   Oh, come on, you know we didn't have the chance. You sent it right up to the board room.

#2:   Why, because you told me to send it right up when the meeting was pushed to this morning. I rushed to get it done and I guess that's where the mistake happened.

#1:   I know but you shouldn't have been rushed. The report should have been finished days ago. Now, to answer your question as to why the CEO didn't look at the full report, he doesn't have time. They were discussing several companies, and in the preliminary stages they look at the bottom line – the total suggested purchase price. The one at the bottom of the summary sheet. The one in your report that read 170 million!

#2:   What happened?

#1:   Farady made it to the meeting, but late. When he asked about Mitchell Industries, they told him it was a no go because it was too expensive, he looked at the report then pointed out the mistake. To say the very least our CEO was not pleased with the error.

#2:   So what are you saying? He wants my head?

#1:   Actually he wants your head, your feet, and everything in between. And Farady's – going to give it to him.

#2:   *(Is in shock.)* No! You can't let them fire me for a...typing mistake.

#1:   Oh please, we're not talking about not dotting an i or crossing a T here. This is major. It's a screw-up that can't be ignored.

#2: OK, but it's still only one screw-up.

#1: I wish I could say that were the case.

#2: What are you saying?

#1: I'm saying that according to your latest evaluation, your performance has been — borderline at best.

#2: I haven't been here all that long. I'm still learning the ropes.

#1: After six months that might be true, but you've been here nine. The ropes should all be familiar by now.

#2: So, care to tell me about all those other hideous mistakes I've made?

#1: Now, don't get like that. That's not what I said. What I've been told is that you're generally — sloppy, not exact in your work. There are lots of little things that by themselves are nothing, but together don't paint a very flattering, larger picture.

#2: Or one of continuing employment.

#1: I'm afraid not.

#2: You know what really stinks about all this? I've really been trying. I've never been late, I don't leave early...

#1: True, you were here exactly at nine and left exactly at six.

#2: You make that sound like a crime.

#1: Then you're not hearing me. What I'm saying is you did what was expected. You never put in even a little extra effort. Effort that may have been beneficial.

#2: How? By giving me more time to brown nose?

#1: No, by giving you extra time to work on your computer skills, or learn new programs faster. Maybe get a jump on the day's work. Who knows, maybe you wouldn't have been behind on the Mitchell Industries report and made the mistake.

#2: So you're saying the whole Mitchell Industries thing is my fault?

#1: Yes, yes I am. And you know it, too.

#2:   What the hell am I supposed to do now? I needed this job. It's not like I had the chance to put any money away. It took me nine months of employment just to get out of debt. And now I have to look for another job?

#1:   You'll get a severance and maybe we can help with a new job...

#2:   How? Are you going to write me a recommendation letter? I can see that now, "I highly recommend Jeff/Jill for your job opening. He/She is inept, sloppy, lazy and his/her only good quality is that he/she is punctual." No thanks. That kind of help I don't need.

#1:   That's not what I meant and you know it. But if you're intent on making me the bad guy – so be it.

#2:   *(Pause)* I'm sorry. I just don't know what to do.

#1:   If I were you, I'd look for a slow moving job. One that allows you the time to learn and the opportunity to screw up without severe consequences.

#2:   An idiot's job.

#1:   No, just more...entry level. You're not at the level you think you are. That could be your biggest problem.

#2:   Look, I appreciate what you're saying, but can't you just give me another chance? I'll do everything you say. I'll come in early, leave late...I'll try harder.

#1:   I wish I could, but in the long run, it wouldn't be good for you, and it's already not good for us.

#2:   You won't even ask?

#1:   No, I won't. I'm sorry. *(Pause)* You're fired! Please be out by the end of the day. *(#2 stands and exits.)*

50. The Witness

(#1 is walking around a police interrogation room. #2 enters.)

#2: Mr./Ms Kramer, I'm Detective Roth. Why don't you sit down?

#1: I don't feel like sitting down.

#2: OK. Can we get you anything? Coffee, soda, juice?

#1: What I'd like is to get out of here.

#2: I'm afraid that we can't do that. Not just yet.

#1: Why not? I told the other officer that I didn't see anything.

#2: Unfortunately, he didn't believe you.

#1: Well that's too bad! You can't just keep me here.

#2: Yes, we can. We believe that you are a material witness to a homicide, and we can keep you here until we get some answers.

#1: I told you! I didn't...

#2: Look, why don't you just stay calm. Sit down and tell me what happened.

#1: I already told the other cop.

#2: Humor me. Let's take it from the beginning.
(Both sit down at the table.)

#1: OK, I was coming home. I stopped at a convenience store...

#2: The one at Third and Cochran?

#1: You know it was.

#2: Just verifying facts. Was anyone else in the store?

#1: A couple of people.

#2: Go on.

#1: I was getting a soda, someone came in, there was yelling and then I heard some shots. That's when the guy in the blue ski cap ran out.

#2: What guy?

#1: I told the other cop that I saw someone run out!

#2: I know, but you didn't mention the blue ski cap before and...how did you know that the guy in the ski cap came in and wasn't already there.

#1: Because I didn't notice him when I came in.

#2: Oh, so you do notice things like that. See, this is the problem that I'm having. You said you didn't see anything, yet you've just told me two new facts that you didn't mention before.

#1: So?

#2: So, I'm thinking that maybe you remember more than you're telling me.

#1: I really don't care what you're thinking.

#2: You should. Now, did you see the guy in the ski cap come in? If you were getting a soda, as you said, the refrigerator is across from the door with only the check-out counter between you. The clerk remembers you standing there.

#1: Yeah, right! The clerk was in the back room or something during the whole thing. He couldn't have seen me.

#2: Oh that's right...but you noticed the missing clerk. So...maybe you did notice Mr. Ski-cap come in.
(A silence.)

#1: OK, yeah, I guess I saw him come in. But I really didn't take any notice of him.

#2: You didn't take notice?

#1: No, I didn't! What are you saying? Every time you're in a store you can describe everyone who's there or comes in after you?

#2: No, but if a person came in and blew someone's head off, I probably would.

#1: I hit the floor when the shooting started. I was covering my head and praying that I wasn't going to get shot. I really apologize for not taking the time to sketch a picture of the assailant for you.

#2: When did you look up again?

#1: When I heard a car screeching away from the front of the store.

#2: Did you see the car?

#1: Somewhat.

#2: Do you know what kind it was?

#1: *(Pause)* Mustang. Probably sixty-five or sixty-six.

#2: How do you know that?

#1: I recognized the back end. It was black. I used to have the same one.

#2: Now, for the sixty-four-thousand-dollar question. Did you get a license plate number?
(The two stare at each other for a moment.)

#1: I...I don't remember.

#2: Did you get a license plate number?!

#1: I don't remember!

#2: TELL ME!

#1: OK, you want the truth?! Fine! When I looked up, the back end of the car was lit up by the store lights and I saw a license plate. Also, I could probably pick the guy out in a line-up...but I won't.

#2: What do you mean, you won't?

#1: Just that. I won't do it!

#2: Why not?

#1: Why should I? From what I was told it was gang activity. If they want to hurt each other,...whatever.

#2: Well here's a fact you might not know. There was a second person killed in that store. And she wasn't a gang kid. She was a mother just stopping at the store to get her kids some ice cream.

#1: I'm sorry about that, but I don't plan on winding up like she did.

#2: That won't happen.

#1: Really!? *(Tosses #2 the pad that's on the table.)* Go ahead! Put it in writing. Write me a guarantee it won't. Because when I'm lying on the sidewalk in front of my house or on the floor of some store, or slumped over in my car with a bullet in my brain, at least I'll have it on paper that you said it wouldn't happen!

#2:   If you help us we can nail this guy and put him away. He won't be able to hurt you.

#1:   Do you see moron written on my forehead? What, he doesn't have friends? He won't have gang buddies sitting in the courtroom looking at me and...and following me everywhere until they can get a clear shot?

#2:   *(Pause)* We will do everything we can to protect you. You'll have a twenty-four-hour guard.

#1:   For how long? Forever? Sooner or later you'll leave and these guys have a long memory...and you know it.

#2:   We'll do everything we can.

#1:   That's not good enough. Forget it!

#2:   This is what really makes me mad. Everyone's upset about all the violence out there and you have a chance to do something about it.

#1:   Hey, I didn't ask for this!

#2:   Who does? But the facts are, it happened, you were there, and what the hell are you going to do about it?

#1:   I don't plan on doing anything!
      (A pause.)

#2:   Then there's nothing else I can do. *(#1 gets up and starts to leave.)* I want you to remember something, though. This kid killed two people tonight. He's probably killed before and will almost definitely kill again. And when he does, it's going to be partially your fault, because you could have helped put him away.

#1:   You can't lay that on me.

#2:   I'm just stating facts...and you know what I'm saying is true. If you can live with that – more power to you. Now, you can go.
      (#1 starts to head out, stops and turns back to #2.)

215

#1: Look I'll give you the license and if you get him, I'll pick him out of a line-up, but I don't want to testify.

#2: We'll do everything we can. Who knows, maybe he'll cop to a plea.

#1: I hope so. *(Walks back to the table and sits down.)*

#2: You're doing the right thing.

#1: Just keep telling me that. OK, the license is...
(They talk.)

About the Author

Garry Kluger was born in Baltimore, Maryland and started acting in theatre at the age of eight. Since moving to Los Angeles, he has appeared in close to twenty films and television shows, and more than fifty plays, both popular and classic.

Garry's writing includes his first book, *Original Auditions Scenes for Actors,* which won an award in 1988, scripts for television, movie reviews, magazine articles, and three plays. His first play, *Till Death, or Whatever, Do Us Part*, had its world premiere in Los Angeles in 1992 and is currently in print. His other two plays are at various stages of development at this time. They are *Office Hours* and *In A Yellow Wood.* Garry, along with his wife Lori, are the head writers and story editors for an award-winning Discovery Channel show titled, *The Ultimate Guide.*